D1632908

IT-Enabled Business Change

Change

Successful Management

The British Computer Society

BCS is the leading professional body for the IT industry. With members in over 100 countries, the BCS is the professional and learned Society in the field of computers and information systems.

The BCS is responsible for setting standards for the IT profession. It is also leading the change in public perception and appreciation of the economic and social importance of professionally managed IT projects and programmes. In this capacity, the Society advises, informs and persuades industry and government on successful IT implementation.

IT is affecting every part of our lives and that is why the BCS is determined to promote IT as the profession of the 21st century.

Joining BCS

BCS qualifications, products and services are designed with your career plans in mind. We not only provide essential recognition through professional qualifications but also offer many other useful benefits to our members at every level.

BCS Membership demonstrates your commitment to professional development. It helps to set you apart from other IT practitioners and provides industry recognition of your skills and experience. Employers and customers increasingly require proof of professional qualifications and competence. Professional membership confirms your competence and integrity and sets an independent standard that people can trust. Professional Membership (MBCS) is the pathway to Chartered IT Professional (CITP) Status.
www.bcs.org/membership

Further Information

Further information about BCS can be obtained from: The British Computer Society, First Floor, Block D, North Star House, North Star Avenue, Swindon, SN2 1FA, UK.
Telephone: 0845 300 4417 (UK only) or + 44 (0)1793 417 424 (overseas)
Contact: www.bcs.org/contact

IT-Enabled Business Change

Successful Management

Sharm Manwani

 BCS

The British Computer Society
Publishing and Information Products
First Floor, Block D
North Star House
North Star Avenue
Swindon
SN2 1FA
UK

www.bcs.org

ISBN 978-1-902505-91-6

British Cataloguing in Publication Data.
A CIP catalogue record for this book is available at the British Library.

Typeset by Lapiz Digital Services
Printed at Antony Rowe.

Contents

List of figures and tables

Author

Dr Sharm Manwani is an Associate Professor at Henley Business School where he researches, lectures and manages programmes in IT-Enabled Business Change. Prior to this, he held several leadership positions with multinational companies most recently as Vice-President, IT & Business Processes at Electrolux Europe.

During his career, Sharm has successfully led a large number of major international IT change programmes. These included mergers, acquisitions, cross-border shared services, business process re-engineering, enterprise resource planning and IT restructuring.

Sharm provides consultancy to leading companies on Strategy, IT Leadership and Programme Management. He is a Fellow of the British Computer Society and a judge for major IT awards. Contact him at Sharm@Manwani.co.uk.

Note: As of August 2008, Henley Management College merged with the business school of the University of Reading to create the Henley Business School at the University of Reading.

Foreword

Technical innovations have changed complete political, social and economical systems in history several times. Taking a closer look at these fundamental changes, there are a few interesting things to notice.

Firstly, technical inventions were the base for the innovation and even change-resistant critics were unable to hold up the resulting fundamental and global change. Secondly, at the heart of most changes were real innovations, not just new ideas. A real innovation is characterised by a new idea or technology commercialised and implemented as a sustainable business. Thirdly, at the beginning of these innovations, there were no 'business cases' for any of them. Bell thought that there was no global application of electrical lighting, as one needed power plants, electrical networks and bulb manufacturing and none were available as commodities, as they are today. The global market for computers was estimated as a maximum of five, when IBM developed the first programmable electrical machines. Later in the 1990s people said that there would be no mass market for mobile phones as they cost US$20,000, weighed 10 kilos and network coverage was spotty. Today billions of people use this technology globally and a multitude of completely new industries and business models have emerged successfully and there are many more to come.

With the advent of the information age another important aspect becomes increasingly important when looking at business ideas: the external network effect. This is where the utility of an item grows proportionally or sometimes even exponentially with the number of its users. This is best understood with telephones. Just imagine the utility of a phone if there is only one, there are two or everyone has one. The same is true for many new business models such as eBay or Google. This can be helpful in understanding the enormous market capitalisations of such companies.

Today IT has become the nervous system of any business, industry, enterprise or company. The better this system works, the better the company can compete in its markets. The system, however, is not a purpose by itself. When managing IT one must understand that there are areas with different characteristics that must be treated adequately and not mingled together.

There is the area that I would call 'non-discretionary'. Here major innovations are mostly over and everyone has access to best practice. The only way to differentiate in this area is by cost-efficiency. Systems stability, reliability, cost per transaction and units consumed are the main drivers and are undeniably very important in any IT manager's life and the basis for everything else. Unfortunately, this is the area most business managers see to be IT's main and often only domain. Hence they try to manage it through key figures such as IT-spend as a percentage of revenues. While focus on cost is important in this area, one also needs to take technological change, new functionalities, maintenance etc. into account and install a good and strict prioritisation and technology refresh process. This must be imbedded with the normal resource and finance planning process of the company and led by the IT group. We also speak about this area as 'run the company'.

The much more important and also interesting area is the one I would call 'discretionary' and which is often referred to as 'change the company'. This is the area where innovations are formed. New technological possibilities mix with new business ideas in a constant and iterative innovation process between the IT organisation and the business functions. Remembering the characteristics of fundamental and sustainable change we spoke of above, this process is a very entrepreneurial one, often involving the Boards of Management and Directors of companies because of its all-encompassing nature. To drive or at least to be part of this process is the most interesting and creative task of IT and the one that makes the difference between being a 'Director of IT' and a real 'Chief Information Officer' (CIO). To accomplish this, IT managers need a fundamental and deep under-standing not only of technology and its application, but also the industry they are in, the traditional and emerging business functions and the economical models behind all these. The latter is most important as, in this discretionary area, IT is competing head-on with other business functions on a short- and long-term basis for funds out of the free cash flow of the enterprise. Sometimes this will mean considering major investments with multi-year business cases necessitating external funding.

Becoming much more of a business enabler than a mere company backbone operator is the challenge of any CIO and IT organisation. How well IT lives up to this challenge will determine its position within the enterprise and its ability to add sustainable innovation to the business.

A core capability to master this challenge is a structured communication process between business and IT. This book brings you ideas, frameworks and processes to be more successful in understanding, mastering and leading this important communication with your business counterparts. I wish you lots of pleasure and success in navigating technological and business change, improving and innovating your business through IT.

Peter Thomas Sany

Peter Sany has been Group Chief Information Officer at Deutsche Telekom since September 2005 when the post was created, and is responsible for information management and processes. The Deutsche Telekom Group has 2007 revenues in excess of 60 billion euros with 244,000 employees.

Acknowledgements

Many parties have contributed to the development and production of this book. My career as a practitioner and manager has evolved into a portfolio of academic, professional and consulting roles. This has provided me with access to a network of information systems professionals, executives and organisations as shown below.

THE BRITISH COMPUTER SOCIETY

The British Computer Society (BCS) promotes professionalism in many guises, including the Professionalism in IT programme (Prof IT) sponsored by David Clarke and led by Colin Thompson. As an Executive Board member of Prof IT I have seen at first hand the commitment from BCS to work with a range of industry partners to create a business-driven and professional approach to IT.

BCS promotes a range of qualifications. The development of the IT-enabled business change qualification was a key driver behind this book. Matthew Flynn, the BCS editor, has provided valuable guidance at every stage of the creation of this book.

ISEB QUALIFICATION WORKING PARTY

Members of a specially formed ISEB working party generated the contents of the IT-enabled business change qualification. Included in this book are some of the outputs of this work, most notably the sample questions, glossary of terms and the core IT-enabled business change life cycle model. The working party comprised Karen Webb from BCS with a selected team of Peter Hardie-Bick, Debbie Paul, Darren Scates, Paul Turner and myself.

INDUSTRY FRAMEWORKS

The Skills Framework for the Information Age (SFIA) provides a framework for the identification of the skills needed to develop and operate effective information systems (IS). The SFIA Foundation comprises: e-skills UK – The Sector Skills Council for IT and Telecoms, BCS, The Institution of

Engineering and Technology and The Institute for the Management of Information Systems. Permission has kindly been granted to use extracts from SFIA with support from Ron McLaren.

The Office of Government Commerce (OGC) is an office of HM Treasury, responsible for improving value for money in procurement. One of the ways it increases capability is through developing useful frameworks for programme management. Permission has been granted to produce selected extracts and references with support from Bob Assirati.

CASE ORGANISATIONS

Practical experiences reinforce the theory of a professional or academic qualification. I am grateful to senior IT executives such as Ailsa Beaton from the Metropolitan Police Service and Phil Ives from Yell for sharing their insights to provide both a public and private sector view. I have also included examples from my own experiences as a leader of IT-enabled business change in large multinational companies.

OTHER INFLUENCERS

Many others have influenced this work. The reviewers of this book provided very helpful feedback, with Jackie Shearer and Paul Turner providing additional considered and constructive comments. I have worked closely with colleagues developing material for the MBA programme at Henley Management College including Peter Race, Chris Head and many others. Tim O'Leary and I conducted research into leading IT-enabled business change supported by the Change Leadership Network led by Jean Irvine, OBE, and Serco. Finally, my thanks to all those whom I have not explicitly named but who have directly or indirectly influenced the contents of this book.

Abbreviations

BCS	British Computer Society
BPO	Business process outsourcing
BPR	Business process redesign
CATWOE	Customer, actor, transformation, Weltanschauung, owner, environmental constraints
CIO	Chief information officer
COTS	Commercial off the shelf
CSF	Critical success factor
DSDM	Dynamic Systems Development Method
EA	Enterprise architecture
EIP	Executive information planning
ERP	Enterprise resource planning
HR	Human Resources
IMP	Information Management Profession (group)
IT	Information technology
ITIL	IT Infrastructure Library
KPI	Key performance indicator
MOST	Mission, objectives, strategy, tactics
MPS	Metropolitan Police Service
NPfIT	National Programme for IT
NPV	Net present value
OGC	Office of Government Commerce
PEST	Political, economic, sociological, technological
PESTLE	Political, economic, sociological (social, socio-cultural), technological, legal, environmental
PID	Project initiation document
PIR	Post-implementation review
PRINCE2®	Projects In a Controlled Environment

Prof IT	Professionalism in IT programme
RAD	Rapid Application Development
RFC	Requests for change
ROI	Return on investment
SARAH	Shock, anger, rejection, acceptance, hope
SDLC	Systems development life cycle
SFIA	Skills Framework for the Information Age
SRO	Senior responsible owner
SRO/PO	Senior responsible owner/project owner
SSADM	Structured Systems Analysis and Design Method
SSM	Soft systems methodology
SWOT	Strengths, weaknesses, opportunities, threats
TOGAF	The Open Group Architecture Framework

Glossary

This Glossary was compiled by members of the ISEB IT-Enabled Business Change qualification working party.

Activity sampling An investigation technique carried out to determine the amount of time individuals spend on different aspects of their work. This approach involves the collection of data that may be used for statistical analysis.

Application life cycle The approach taken to the management and control of all application-related activities and information over the application and asset life cycle. This includes both the development or acquisition of the application, its customisation and integration, its delivery and subsequent support and management as a service to the business.

Balanced scorecard A balanced business scorecard supports a strategic management system by capturing both financial and non-financial measures of performance.

Benefits realisation A process that is concerned with achieving the business benefits predicted in the business case for a change project. This process requires a focus on business benefits throughout the business change life cycle and includes managing the project in order to deliver the predicted benefits and, after the project has been implemented, checking progress on the achievement of such benefits and taking any actions required to support their delivery.

Business actor Those individuals or groups who have an interest in, or may be affected by, the business change project.

Business activity model A diagrammatic representation of a business area showing business activities, business events and business rules. An example is that used within the Soft Systems Method. It represents a future view of the activities necessary for the business to achieve its perceived objectives and takes account of a range of perspectives as to what these activities might be.

Business analysis An internal consultancy specialism that has the responsibility for investigating business situations, identifying options for improving business systems and bridging the needs of the business with the use of IT.

Business capability The skills and capacity of an organisation to effectively operate one or more business processes.

Business case   The presentation of a proposal describing the significant aspects that could influence a decision to proceed with an initiative. It would normally include: an introduction, management summary, description of the current situation, options considered, analysis of costs and benefits, impact assessment, risk assessment, recommendations, appendices including detailed supporting information.

Business change life cycle   The different stages of organisational change covering alignment, improvement, design, implementation and benefits.

Business change management   The process of managing the organisation through the business change life cycle.

Business continuity   Business continuity describes the processes and procedures an organisation puts in place to ensure that essential functions can continue during and after a disaster. Business continuity planning seeks to prevent interruption of mission-critical services and to re-establish full functioning as swiftly and smoothly as possible.

Business environment   The external environment that is the source of forces that may impact a business organisation. Types of forces may be the introduction of new laws, social trends or competitor actions. See **PESTLE analysis**.

Business intelligence   Information that is used to manage the business of an organisation derived both from analysing operational data and acquiring external information.

Business process modelling   A technique for producing a diagrammatic representation of the steps that need to be carried out in order to respond to a business event or trigger and achieve a specific goal or objective.

Business process   Any set of tasks performed by a business that is initiated by an event, that transforms information, real-world items or business commitments, and produces an output. This output should be valued by customers or by other processes.

Business requirements elicitation   The investigation and collection of requirements for an IT solution required to resolve a business problem or enable a business opportunity.

Business rule   A business rule specifies how an organisation will operate in specific circumstances. For example, it will perform a credit check on all new customers to verify that they do not have a bad credit history.

Business sponsor   A senior person in an organisation who is accountable for delivering the benefits from a business change.

Business strategy A strategy describes the approach and decisions taken to achieve the goals of an organisation.

Business user The set of actors or roles in a business change project from the customer side of the equation. It covers from sponsor through domain experts to the actual end users of any solution.

Change control A process whereby changes to requirements are handled in a controlled fashion. This process will ensure that any proposed change is analysed to determine the impact of the change. Following this analysis, a formal decision is made, and recorded, about the action to be taken with regard to the proposed change.

Change management The different stages of organisational performance resulting from the implementation issues and psychological responses which follow a significant change.

Core competency A core competency is a business capability that provides customer benefits, is difficult for competitors to imitate and contributes to many products or markets.

Cost-benefit analysis This is a process identifying where initial and ongoing costs will be incurred and where both financial and non-financial benefits can reasonably be expected.

Critical success factors These are the limited number of areas in which positive results will ensure successful organisational performance.

Cultural factors These define the values and behaviours of an organisation or a geographical region.

Data warehouse A data warehouse is where large quantities of data are collected together from a variety of locations for efficient analysis; it also provides a form of archive of the data. Since the data is likely only to be used for further analysis it does not have to be complete or up to date.

Deliverables A deliverable is a tangible component of a project which can be declared to be unambiguously complete (or not). All projects should have deliverables that define the completion of the project. Projects may also require the production of intermediate deliverables which are necessary to produce the final end result. Deliverables provide a basis for project estimating, planning, monitoring and control.

Development life cycle A conceptual model that describes the stages involved in an information system development project, from an initial feasibility study to maintenance of the completed application. Various approaches have been developed to guide the processes involved, including the waterfall model, the V-Model and rapid application development/Agile (based on an incremental and iterative approach). Frequently several of these are combined into some sort of hybrid method. Documentation is crucial regardless of the type of model chosen or devised for any application, and is usually done in parallel with the development process. Some methods work better for specific types of project.

Enterprise architecture A framework that maps and integrates processes, information, applications and technology in support of business goals.

Enterprise resource planning An integrated set of applications that supports the operational business processes of an organisation.

Ethnographic study An ethnographic study is concerned with spending an extended period of time in an organisation in order to obtain a detailed understanding of the culture and behaviours of the business area under investigation.

External business environment See **Business environment**

Force field analysis Force field analysis provides a framework for looking at the factors (forces) that influence any given situation. It looks at forces that are either driving movement toward a goal (helping forces) or blocking movement toward a goal (hindering forces). Developed by Kurt Lewin, it is a significant contribution to the fields of organisational development and process management. It is a method for analysing change and is used in change management.

Gap analysis Gap analysis concerns the comparison of two views of a business system, the current and the 'ideal' or required view, in order to determine where the current situation has 'gaps'. This leads to the identification of actions to improve the situation. The business activity modelling technique may be used to provide an ideal view that can then be compared with a view of the current situation. An alternative approach is to use the business process modelling technique, using 'as is' and 'to be' process models.

Holistic approach The consideration of all aspects of a business system – the people, process and organisational areas – in addition to the technology.

Incremental approach   The delivery of a developed or procured software solution in phases with each phase adding additional functionality or performance.

Information   Data organised and arranged in a manner that conveys meaning both to its use in context and in relation to other data.

Intangible cost   A cost incurred by a business change project for which a credible monetary value cannot be predicted.

Internal business environment   The internal factors that affect an organisation's ability to respond to external environment forces. An analysis of the mission, objectives, strategy and tactics set out by its directors (MOST analysis) and a consideration of the physical, financial and human resources available to the organisation will help develop an understanding of the strengths and weaknesses of the organisation.

IT-enabled business change   The improvements in the way an organisation carries out its business brought about through the effective use of information technology.

IT architecture   IT architecture has two meanings depending upon its contextual usage: (i) a formal description of an IT system, or a detailed plan of the system at component level to guide its implementation; (ii) the structure of IT components, their interrelationships and the principles and guidelines governing their design and evolution over time.

IT governance   IT governance is the accountability framework that ensures executive and management responsibility for the effective business-aligned development and use of IT and the appropriate moderation of IT risks.

Key performance indicators   These are financial and non-financial metrics used to quantify objectives to reflect the strategic performance of an organisation.

Management consultant   An individual experienced in managerial practices who is able to support business managers in their work.

Management information   See **Business intelligence**

MOST analysis   An analysis of the mission, objectives, strategy and tactics to identify any strengths or weaknesses inherent in the organisation, for example from a lack of strategic direction or unclear objectives. See **Internal business environment**.

OGC OGC is an independent office of the Treasury that works with public sector organisations to help them improve their efficiency, gain better value for money from their commercial activities and deliver improved success from programmes and projects. As part of this it has produced a range of best practice guidance and publications, including PRINCE2 and ITIL.

Option in a business case The first step in developing a business case is to identify (in the case of IT business cases) two types of option: (i) business options – explore what the proposed solution is intended to achieve in business terms; (ii) technical options – consider how the solution is to be implemented most probably in terms of IT.

Organisation structure Typically this will be a diagram showing the departments and personnel as a hierarchy within an organisation. It may, however, be developed to show more detail about the responsibilities and procedures carried out by departments, sections and personnel.

Organisational boundary The definition of the scope of an organisation showing where the interactions occur between the organisation itself and its customers, partners and suppliers.

Organisational capability See **Business capability**

Outsourcing The process of selecting external suppliers in preference to in-house resources, with the capability to provide effective IT services to meet overall organisation goals and strategy.

Performance measurement Measures that enable management to monitor the success of specific units or entities within an organisation. These measures may be quantitative, not necessarily financial, or qualitative when relating to human performance of significant tasks.

PESTLE An analysis of the political, economic, sociological (social, socio-cultural), technological, legal and environment forces that may impact upon an organisation. See **Business environment**.

Post-implementation review One or more reviews held periodically after project closure to determine whether the expected benefits have been obtained.

Programme A collection of projects that is directed toward a common goal.

Programme manager See **Programme management**.

Programme management The overall management of a programme through a set of projects while ensuring continued alignment to the programme goals.

Project A project is a set of activities with a defined start point and defined end state, which pursues a defined goal and uses a defined set of resources.

Project initiation document A document that identifies the customer for the project and clarifies the objectives, scope, deliverables, timescale and available resources.

Project sponsor See **Business sponsor**.

Risk management The monitoring and controlling of significant risks during the development, design and implementation of IT systems.

SARAH The psychological states that an individual is likely to go through when faced with major unplanned change from an external source: shock, anger, rejection, acceptance, hope.

SFIA and SFIA Plus SFIA is the Skills Framework for the Information Age. SFIA Plus includes additional detail. These are standard frameworks for the definition of skills in the information systems field.

SMART A mnemonic used to ensure that objectives are clearly defined in that they are specific, measurable, achievable, relevant and time-framed.

Soft systems methodology An approach to analysing business situations devised by Peter Checkland and his team at Lancaster University.

Software package Often referred to as COTS (commercial off the shelf), a software package is a purchased solution to a business problem rather than a bespoke development.

Stakeholder Someone with an interest in the change. Categories may include: customers, employees, managers, partners, regulators, owners, suppliers, contractors.

Stakeholder analysis Consideration of their power and interests is a way of categorising stakeholders that acts as a guide for engagement to achieve buy-in to the desired change.

Stakeholder management The process of analysing and engaging with stakeholders.

Strategic analysis The consideration of an organisation and its strategic position in the light of its external business environment and internal capability.

Strategy   The direction and scope of an organisation over the long term. The strategy is defined in order to achieve competitive advantage for the organisation through its configuration of resources within a changing business environment. The strategy also needs to fulfil the stakeholders' expectations.

Swimlanes   A row on a business process diagram or model. A way of indicating who is responsible for a given process or task. In most cases swimlanes are assigned to departments, groups within department, individuals, applications, systems of applications or databases.

SWOT analysis   An approach to analysing the strategy of an organisation. Consideration of the strengths, weaknesses, opportunities and threats provides a framework for strategic analysis.

Systemic view   An approach that views a business situation as a system of related activities in order to analyse the situation and identify opportunities for business improvement.

Task modelling   The technique for developing a model which describes the human activities and task sequences required by a business system. The task model elaborates the tasks identified by mapping business processes onto specific individuals or workgroups.

TOWS analysis   An approach to analysing the strategy of an organisation. Consideration of the threats, opportunities, weaknesses and strengths provides a framework for strategic analysis. See **SWOT analysis**.

Work practice modelling   The definition of user roles and the classification of users, via user analysis, so that job design can be carried out in support of the IT activities within a task.

1 Introduction

Nothing endures but change.
Heraclitus, from Diogenes Laertius, Lives of Eminent Philosophers
Greek philosopher (540 BC–480 BC)

CONTEXT

Change happens in organisations. Sometimes you have a choice – to be in the driving seat, ride as a passenger or not to get onto the bus. At other times that choice is made for you. When it comes to business change you may be asked to lead a major project or to join the team. Alternatively you may be the recipient of change (or unaffected by it).

This book is about business change in organisations. It examines why organisations change the way they work. It looks at how change is managed through projects. It considers the impact and reliance on people to do things differently. The focus is on a particular type of business change, one that involves the use of information technology (IT).

What is IT-enabled business change?

IT-enabled business change is a term that denotes a mix of two very different elements – IT and business change. Why is this term more appropriate than 'IT project'? The label of 'IT project' is arguably simpler and descriptive since projects deliver change and IT describes the type of solution. However, calling it an IT project implies an over-dependent focus on the technology part of the solution. In contrast, 'business change' makes it clear that the focus is on a change in the business activities of an organisation which may or may not be enabled by IT. The term 'IT-enabled business change' reflects a type of hybrid change as represented in Figure 1.1.

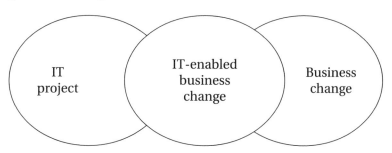

FIGURE 1.1 *IT-enabled business change*

There are business change projects such as introducing an employee suggestion and reward scheme which have few or no elements of IT. At the other extreme there are (apparently) fully IT projects such as the introduction of an IT computer network to link together two sites. With a wider view, however, this might in practice be an IT-enabled business change requiring many staff movements and training to enable communications between the personnel in these sites.

Many initiatives or projects that are or should be an IT-enabled business change are incorrectly labelled as IT projects. This is often true of commentary on national government projects that spend vast amounts of money on new IT systems due to the scale of the change. The visibility of both the IT spend and the failure to deliver if the system is late makes this type of project a strong contender for media attention. Below is an example of one such report and there are many others in the public domain.

'NEW IT PROGRAMME CRASHES'

This was the headline report in a national UK newspaper about the halting of development work on a £244 million UK programme designed to create a single, accurate profile of an offender. It was said that the original costing had been 'optimistic' and a fundamental review was needed to 'return to an affordable programme'. The failure of this programme was set in the context of a range of other public sector programmes, which included:

- cost of IT systems for magistrates courts rises from £146m to £232m;
- IT systems for asylum applications abandoned after £77m contract fails to deliver;
- a £1bn IT project to create a swipe card capability collapses.

Source: *The Times*, 9 August 2007

In these cases, there are usually some business change impacts that have not been properly considered, which emerge through a more detailed analysis of the issues. This is illustrated by reports on one of the most costly and wide-ranging IT-enabled business change programmes of all time – the National Health Service (NHS) implementation of new systems in the UK, called NPfIT (National Programme for IT). Below is an extract of an article on the interim report from the National Audit Office which examines these types of programme, effectively on behalf of the taxpayer.

UK NATIONAL HEALTH SERVICE PROGRAMME

The committee's report – drafted initially by the National Audit Office – depicts the NPfIT as a failure so far. It also finds that the programme might have done more harm than good, by inhibiting innovation and progress. The strongest criticisms are in the final paragraph. It simply questions whether the 10-year contracts – which could cost taxpayers £6.2bn – will bring significant clinical benefits by the time they expire. This report derived the following apposite conclusion.

The programme has 'focused too narrowly on the delivery of IT systems at the expense of the proper consideration of how best to use IT within a broader process of business change'.

Source: *Computer Weekly,* 17 April 2007

In other reports on this programme, concern was expressed at the lack of engagement with medical staff in designing and communicating the changes in the way they were expected to work as a result of new integrated appointments and record-keeping systems.

Why is IT-enabled business change important?

These days much of the change in organisations is enabled by IT. Why is this so? A key reason is that the activities of a commercial organisation rely on IT to implement the business rules which define how an organisation operates in its environment. These rules relate to business processes that are sets of activities to support a customer. One such example is the order to payment process, which starts with a customer need and ends with the cash in the bank. It covers the activities of taking orders from the customer, delivering products, invoicing customers and receiving the payment, as shown in Figure 1.2.

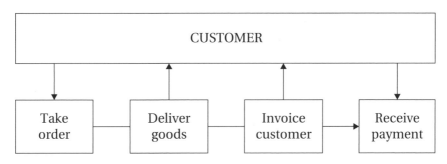

FIGURE 1.2 *Business process*

A commercial organisation will want to manage the risk that its customers are not able to pay the invoice. Hence it may create a business rule, which applies when it takes an order, to carry out a check that the total amount outstanding is less than the agreed credit limit. This check is usuallycarried out using a computer system where the limit has been pre-defined by a credit controller. If an organisation wishes to change the business rule either the data or the system, or both, must be updated. The way this type of change is managed not only affects the current way of doing business but if badly handled may have an adverse impact on future changes over many years.

There are very many business rules in a large organisation; far too many for one person to know in detail. If these rules are not well documented, the only place they are made explicit may be in the IT system, which will make the planning of business change more difficult. While processes are often similar, organisations typically have different ways of doing business, hence the use of IT will vary. This way of doing business will change over time. How easy or difficult that change will be often depends on how well the IT system has been designed and implemented in the past. The demand from business executives is for increased agility from their IT systems and business processes.

AGILITY

Phil Ives is the UK head of information services at Yell, a leader in the international directories business. He defines agility as 'being one step ahead of what the business needs'. This is a big challenge in a fast moving business. Phil Ives recognises that this requires strong governance processes combined with responsive people and flexible IT systems.

What is the state of play?

It is often reported that the majority of IT projects are failures. This of course depends on how you measure success and failure. The Standish Group studied more than 40,000 projects in a period of over 10 years[1]. It differentiates between a project being a failure and projects being 'challenged', which means that they are over time, over budget or lacking critical features based on the requirements. There has been a reduction in failure of the average IT projects over time but large IT projects, or, more accurately, IT-enabled business change projects, are still prone to major delays or budget over-runs.

Partly this lack of success is due to the complexity of what is in effect a large engineering project with many different IT components. It is a mistake, however, to focus only on these IT aspects of change. Much of the difficulty in large projects relates to deciding what business change is needed and dealing with the people issues such as engagement and training. In these circumstances, good practice is to treat these as business (change) projects with IT as one of the key enablers.

Business change is not a smooth sequential process. There is, however, a goal to move from an idea to an implementation of that idea. This involves several stages, which include strategic alignment and definition of the required improvement before designing and implementing a business solution, which generates the target benefits. These stages are often iterative as learning from one stage uncovers the need to revise the outputs of a previous stage.

OUTCOMES

What does this book attempt to do?

Awareness of the impact of unsuccessful projects that depend on IT has spread well beyond the computing journals. In the UK, USA and other countries many government programmes have come under intense scrutiny and the public are questioning how their tax contributions are being spent. There have been some high profile failures in the private sector so this is certainly not just an issue for the public sector and government.

The main desired outcome of this book is that it helps those who are involved in IT-enabled business change projects to understand the issues and to be more successful. A caveat is that each project is different hence there are no magic formulas and no guarantees. What can be done is to capture and share good practice using a consistent terminology which becomes familiar to all those involved in IT-enabled change.

Who is this book designed to help?

Anyone who works in an organisation today is likely to be affected by IT-enabled business change. If you understand what is happening, you will be in a better position to judge which bus, or which part of the bus, you would like to be on (if you have the choice). There are many different potential groupings of roles required in IT-enabled business change. One view of these is represented in Figure 1.3, a framework derived from research into the business leadership of IT-enabled change sponsored by the Change Leadership Network.

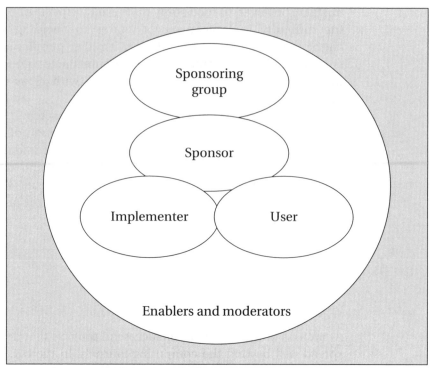

Source: O'Leary and Manwani (2006)[2]

FIGURE 1.3 *IT-enabled business change roles*

Let us start with the implementers. There are some individuals and teams who are directly engaged with implementing IT-enabled change. Business analysts and consultants typically have a very direct role in analysing, designing and implementing IT-enabled business change. They may have come up through the IT or the business route. In either case they need to understand the whole life cycle from both perspectives, which represents a significant challenge that this book aims to address. IT professionals and managers working on projects that implement change also need this full understanding.

IT professionals, suppliers and consultants who work in a specialist area of IT sometimes have difficulty in understanding where they fit into the overall life cycle of change. For example, someone working on an IT helpdesk may be supporting business staff on how to use a new system. Understanding IT-enabled business change will give them insights into the challenges that users face beyond the technology itself. This book will help IT specialists to gain insights into how the different disciplines of service management, project management and business change management are interrelated.

Business sponsors of change are typically senior executives who understand the organisation and the challenges but may have limited direct experience of IT-enabled change programmes. This book describes the role of the sponsor and the key challenges they face over the life of a programme. It will help those who take on this role or are asked to sit on a steering or sponsoring group overseeing the change.

On the user side, business managers may be asked to be change agents and operate in the role of business change managers. They need to work closely with their IT colleagues in achieving the programme goals. In some organisations this is a specialist role of change management working with operational managers to design and implement new processes. A goal of this book is to help them understand what contributions are required in each stage of the IT-enabled change life cycle.

Business actors are individuals or groups who have an interest in, or may be affected by, the business change project. Experienced business actors often take on a role as 'super users' in a project helping in analysing and testing business changes. This book aims to provide insights into what is happening around them and how to influence the outcomes.

There are roles that can be described as enablers and moderators that are important to the success of IT-enabled business change but may not be involved in specific change projects. Chief information officers (CIOs) and heads of IT need to evaluate how IT-enabled change is delivered in their organisations in order to decide what skills are required and where they should be located. These skills are not exclusively in the IT department but a broader organisation view is required for success, and if these business change skills are missing there will be an impact on the perceived capability of the CIO.

Also in this category are the chief executive and the top team. They may not need to understand the specific technology used in their organisation but they should certainly define the governance for IT-enabled business change and drive the business benefits. These are key elements of the preliminary and final stages of the change life cycle.

Given that people and systems are both critical in IT-enabled business change, the involvement of human resource managers is advisable. This is another group located within the 'enablers and moderators' who will benefit from the overview in this book.

In summary this book is aimed at practitioners and consultants directly involved in IT-enabled business change, experienced professionals from IT and other disciplines who work closely with these practitioners and, finally, executives who need to guide one or both of these groups. New entrants to organisations with a related qualification should gain a contextual overview of the subject from this book.

What this book gives you

Chapters in this book follow the IT-enabled business change life cycle. This book provides sample questions for each stage with supporting information to help readers appreciate the reasons for the selected correct answers.

No specific prior knowledge is assumed for this book. The breadth of IT-enabled business change topics covered in this book is necessarily wide given its target positioning. This makes it suitable as an introductory text for qualifications in this area.

Ultimately the book is concerned with the learning of practitioners, executives and advisers in IT-enabled business change and any qualification is a confirmation that a core level of knowledge has been achieved. The working party who designed the outputs to support a qualification as described in the *Acknowledgements* included members with many years of relevant practitioner, consulting and academic experience.

One way that chief information officers (CIOs) can support their organisations in expanding and evidencing the core knowledge in IT-enabled business change is through a relevant qualification. This follows the direction that some CIOs have taken with the Project Management and Service Management qualifications. CIOs have the option to take a leadership role in this type of education throughout the organisation.

Why did I write this book?

The views expressed in this book are based on both theory and practice. My career roles range from business analysis and project management to IT director and CIO. This has given me the opportunity to lead a large number of IT-enabled business projects – big and small. Alongside this I completed my MBA and Doctorate at Henley Management College and then joined the faculty developing and teaching IT-enabled business change courses on the MBA.

One part of my current career portfolio is to advise organisations on strategy, programmes and capability development. I am also committed to developing IT and business change as a professional discipline. In support of this goal, I joined the Executive Board of the Professionalism in IT programme. My other professional activities include writing for practitioner publications such as 'Ask the Experts' in *Computing Business* and the 'Strategy Clinic' in *Computer Weekly*, presenting at conferences and judging at major IT award events.

This breadth and depth of experience provided me with hard-earned lessons and has driven my desire to produce this book. I have included stories from my experiences, which are intended to illustrate the learning. Details have been changed or names excluded to offer anonymity unless permission has been granted for inclusion. My final reason is the evidence that there is a hierarchy of learning that progresses through observing and doing to teaching. I continue to learn about this subject through lecturing, consulting and writing.

FORMAT

How can you use this book?

The proposition is that business change follows a series of stages and this book follows a similar sequence. This means that readers can follow the life cycle of an IT-enabled business change or decide to focus on one particular step such as the implementation of the change. If you decide to implement successful IT-enabled business change you will need a broad understanding of each of the elements and a specific knowledge of the key terms and principles.

Structure

The book has the following main topics:

- Overview of IT-enabled business change.
- Business and IT alignment.
- Business improvement definition.
- Business change design.
- Business change implementation.
- Benefits management.
- Business change and modelling skills and techniques.

The next chapter provides an overview of the life cycle and each of the next five chapters covers a stage of the life cycle. Business change and modelling techniques are summarised in Chapter 7. This book introduces a wide range of concepts and models. It should be recognised that the aim of any model is to provide understanding through an insightful but limited representation of reality. You need to be selective in your use of models. Hence business change and modelling techniques are covered in the most relevant chapters. This does not mean that they can or should only be applied at this stage. In practice, techniques may be appropriate at multiple stages of the business change journey. You will find that many of these models are also referenced in the *Glossary*.

I have worked with many large organisations and consultancies and found that they use a wide variety of models for similar activities such as describing business processes. This book aims to provide a simple representation of some common techniques so that you can start to recognise when these models are appropriate.

Sample questions

The sample questions in this book were developed by an IT-enabled business change working party as described in the *Acknowledgements*. Questions are provided in the relevant chapter. These are all multiple-choice questions. Each of the questions is followed by a discussion that helps to inform the reader which answer is the correct one.

Glossary

The glossary contains many of the key definitions referred to in this book. Some of these definitions are critical to answering the sample questions and these terms will be introduced in the body of this book.

Case stories and study

Practical illustrations are provided through case stories and other relevant material. The main case study is included at the end of the book and is based on a real-life programme with some elements changed to ensure confidentiality. Questions are provided in each chapter to stimulate thinking on the relevant issues that have been introduced through the case study.

Notes

This book is aimed primarily at practitioners and students of IT-enabled business change. The contents cover a broad range of topics. At the end of the book there are opportunities for further reading with references, along with notes, all of which are indicated within the chapters by superscript numbers.

SUMMARY

Projects involving technology have often been viewed as IT projects and the responsibility of the specialist IT function within an organisation. Delivering IT systems has been problematic because of a failure to clearly define the business requirements and a tendency to focus on the system as the deliverable. However, the perception of IT and its value-add is changing significantly in leading organisations. There is a greater acceptance that IT is a means to achieving business improvement rather than an end in itself.

The counterpoint is that much of the creative business change in organisations these days is enabled by IT engineering. There is a powerful but sometimes uncomfortable relationship between these two different worlds. This book aims to provide a methodology and insights for dealing with the opportunities and challenges in this intersection. For those who are interested in a qualification to demonstrate their knowledge and understanding, this book is intended to support relevant courses in IT-enabled business change.

This chapter has introduced many new terms and you may wish to refer to the *Glossary* for further information. At times, this book refers to IT-enabled change; this is used as shorthand for IT-enabled business change.

2 Overview: IT-Enabled Change

'The organisation can use the Benefits Framework to realise the full range of potential offered by the new technology.'

Ailsa Beaton, Director of Information, Metropolitan Police Service
(Case study extract from this chapter)

ROLE OF IT IN ORGANISATIONS

IT-enabled business change, as the name suggests, uses information technology as an enabler to change the way an organisation works. In many organisations today IT is fundamental to **running** the core business operations. Building on this, it is often a key enabler for **improving** business operations. The focus here is on change. That includes changes to business processes to make them more timely and efficient. It covers the provision of enhanced information to support better decision-making. Both these types of improvement in processes and information have the potential to make people more productive. Yet many initiatives labelled as IT projects have repeatedly missed delivery dates, gone well over budget or failed to deliver a working solution to the organisation that realises the intended benefits. Too often the assumption has been that the introduction of IT will deliver the saving; that it is the driver of business improvement. Let us explore how valid this assumption is.

Technology as a driver and enabler of business improvement

Over the last few decades IT has become increasingly important to organisations. It has been a contributor to developing new products, enhancing customer relationships and reducing costs. There is often much debate (and confusion) as to whether IT is a driver or an enabler of business change. If we consider the impact of technology in the last 10 years, we can see how it has driven and enabled business change across a range of industries. In particular, the growth of the internet has allowed organisations to transform the way that they work, most notably through electronic business (e-business) approaches. In many cases this has allowed new industry entrants, without the burden of a legacy sales, operations and IT infrastructure, to create a business that is more competitive than existing organisations. Most people are familiar with the case of Amazon.com, which became the market leader in supplying books by creating a new online books business from scratch. In order to supply products and services in a radically different way, an organisation often needs to redesign its business processes and IT, as shown in the example of Dell.

Personal Computer (PC) industry

> The PC market was originally dominated by companies such as IBM and Compaq. They had extensive dealer networks to distribute the PCs. Dell changed the dynamics of the industry by creating a new build-to-order business model where consumers could order direct from Dell. By not maintaining stocks of finished goods Dell could reduce both their inventory costs and the costs of obsolescence. As a result of this new approach, which aimed to replace inventory with information, Dell became the market leader in the PC industry.

This potential for IT to drive change in organisations is sometimes inappropriately taken to mean that the IT department or system should be put at the forefront of change and that the business should be modified to fit the technology. Instead the need is to understand what opportunities the technology opens up for an organisation, to define the business change that is required and then to use IT as the enabler. The recognition of these two roles of IT – as a driver and an enabler – increases the probability of a successful business change. An understanding of the environmental and industry changes driven by this technology is vital.

IT as a core competence

As a result of changes in technology and industries IT has become a key factor in the business success of many organisations. This does not mean that it plays a strategic role in every organisation but in the vast majority of medium to large organisations it will have a strong operational and support role. Hence it is vital that organisations have the capability to exploit fully the potential that IT offers in relation to what the organisation needs.

One key decision for organisations is how to provide this capability in terms of the mix of external and internal resources. The decision on what to provide internally and what to source externally will depend to some extent on whether the ability to carry out this activity is vital to the success of the organisation. In other words is it viewed by the organisation to be a core competence? If a financial organisation's ability to compete in its marketplace is highly dependent on sophisticated computer software, it is less likely to outsource the software development to a supplier who provides the same facility to the organisation's competitors.

A significant number of large organisations have outsourced part of their IT operations and programming to suppliers in the same country, and in some cases to offshore partners. This growth of outsourcing has enabled many organisations to reduce their IT costs. However, the risk is that it makes it more difficult to make best use of technology where core knowledge has been transferred elsewhere.

Organisations need to ensure that they retain and grow staff with the ability to identify where business change combined with technological developments can benefit the organisation. They also need to consider how they will monitor whether the technology is being managed effectively. Hence several roles related to IT-enabled business change have emerged or grown in importance in the last 5 to 10 years. Some of these are roles within the IT department and some are located in other parts of the organisation. Some are full-time and others are project-related. The level of business and IT knowledge varies across these roles. These roles are examined further in the context of the IT-enabled business change life cycle, which is introduced below.

LIFE CYCLE STAGES

A life cycle has defined start and end points together with intermediate stages. In the case of a product life cycle this covers the process of managing all the stages of a product's life from the original concept through design and manufacture to service and disposal. Investment can take place at any point during the cycle in order to lengthen the life of a product.

In the IT world there is a similar concept known as the systems life cycle or systems development life cycle (SDLC). This starts with the analysis of requirements and ends with the maintenance of the system. A systems development life cycle typically goes through the stages of analysis, design, build, test and implementation. After the implementation the system is then in operation and needs to be maintained for the life of the system. The systems development life cycle focuses on the introduction of a new system and does not directly emphasise the business change and all the components needed to make the business change successful.

IT-enabled business change

The author and members of a working party developed a new life cycle for IT-enabled business change. This life cycle model recognises that the start and end points of the change need to focus on the business goals and the benefits. The first stage is one of strategic alignment that clarifies both the business and the IT goals of the organisation. The final stage is when the benefits from the change have been delivered or assured. Figure 2.1 demonstrates that this is an iterative process with a target direction of travel. Failure is viewed to occur when the anticipated benefits are not realised.

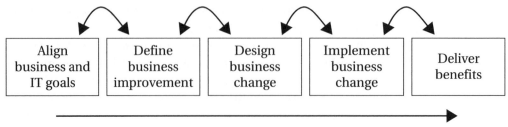

Direction of travel

FIGURE 2.1   *IT-enabled business change life cycle*

Align business and IT goals

A key outcome of this stage is that the organisation aligns its goals with the external environment. Changes to the environment can lead to new ways of doing business within the organisation. Example drivers for change come from a variety of sources such as a new government regulation or the need to respond to a competitive action. These lead to a proposal for business change being put forward. One of the external drivers can be an emerging new technology or there may be an internal driver such as the desire to standardise on a particular IT platform to reduce costs or to enable sharing.

Define business improvement

Based on the broad proposal for change, the business context is investigated in order to identify a series of options and recommendations for the way forward. As a result of this process, a change project is identified that covers many different elements including process, people, information and technology. IT is therefore one enabler for the improvement, such as a new IT call centre system which is combined with telesales rather than selling face-to-face. The need for change is supported by developing a business case.

Design business change

The business change product is designed and developed in this stage. Deliverables from this stage are the design of elements required of the business change product. These include, for example, a set of revised business processes, information updates, new IT software and a training programme. In the case of a new call centre system, the change will not work without the IT software but neither will it be effective if the other components are not fit for purpose.

Implement business change

Implementation of the business change needs a great deal of emphasis on understanding the people who influence or are affected by the change, known as the stakeholders, ensuring that they accept and adapt their ways of working to the new business operation. A communications plan is an important tool to support the buy-in. At the same time, acquisition or development of a new or updated IT system needs to be carefully managed to avoid disruption. Similarly data may need to be created or migrated from the old to the new systems; this is often a risk factor since data quality problems may occur in the transition.

Deliver business benefits

IT is often the enabler of change but it is the business managers who deliver the benefit. This recognition requires us to adopt a different perspective on the planning and running of projects involving IT investment. Achieving the planned benefit is the overriding concern, and this will not happen until the business changes made possible by the implementation of the IT service or application are effected, leading to the delivery of the benefits. A post-implementation review will help to ensure that the IT system is working as required.

AN ILLUSTRATIVE CASE

The progress of the Metropolitan Police Service (MPS) C3i change programme illustrates the five stages of the IT-enabled business change life cycle. C3i is the MPS's biggest-ever organisational change programme. It has redefined the command and control processes, supported by new technologies to ensure that the MPS can provide 21st century, citizen-focused response policing.

Alignment

The C3i Programme was designed to meet the growing demand for MPS services in a complex and evolving environment. Call volumes via the various contact channels are projected to grow to 23 million by 2010. The solutions developed by the C3i Programme have involved the integration of people, processes, information and technology to deliver an effective emergency response 999 service to all those who will live, work, travel in or visit London over the next decade.

The C3i Programme was introduced to ensure that the MPS could continue to provide a robust, sustainable 999 service for London. Public demand for this service was growing while there were on-going financial and resource constraints that needed to be managed. There was a very real risk that this could compromise effective police deployment and place increasing burdens on an ageing infrastructure. At the same time, there was a need to improve customer satisfaction, adopt national standards for call handling and incident reporting and be part of the national initiative to implement a secure radio infrastructure. There were both internal and external drivers for this change.

Improvement

The C3i business improvement objectives were defined as:

- to better manage the demand for a police response;
- to better manage response policing;
- to improve the MPS's call handling and deployment support;
- to make available more police staff for MPS policing priorities.

The C3i Programme required fundamental change for people, processes, information and technology. The programme gathered a unique blend in experience from within the MPS supplemented by experts from the private sector to create a multi-disciplined programme team to manage and deliver this complex programme. The initial analysis highlighted a number of potential options and the final C3i business case was aligned to organisational objectives while responding to external drivers. A formal governance structure was put in place to provide accountability, transparency and ownership.

Design

The C3i Programme design required a mixture of people, processes, information and technology to ensure the management of complex dependencies and seamless integration into the wider MPS environment. It included the development of new business processes for the command and control environment, delivery of a number of major technology projects, provision of timely information, development of three new purpose built command sites, and the transition of over 2000 MPS employees from 33 existing sites across London to three centralised locations.

Crucial to the design was resilience and business continuity: the 999 system is a 24/7/365 service and there could be no downtime during transition to the new way of working. Every aspect of the programme had to integrate with the others – the complex network of interdependencies meant that no single system, process or piece of technology could be introduced independently – not least because they had to fit seamlessly into the wide range of systems and processes the MPS was already using.

Implementation

Because of the complexity of the programme, the MPS focused on proven technology that could be tailored to specific needs. In order to maintain an effective 999 service, each element of the programme was designed to roll out on a phased basis – and to be suspended or rolled back should operational demands make that necessary. Supplier contracts all incorporated rigorous testing and monitoring regimes; and new software was run through 'as-live' and pilot phases before being rolled out. Because of the complexity of the live environment it was accepted that close, proactive monitoring was essential both during and after implementation.

Peaks and troughs in demand from the live environment, training availability, availability of specific skill-sets and recruitment were all issues that impacted implementation. These were mitigated through a robust governance structure and effective working relationships with a wide range of suppliers. The programme also saw implementation as a means to an end, rather than an end in itself.

Benefits

As part of implementation the programme developed a clear 'Benefits Framework' that aligned to the original business case and was supported by carefully monitored key performance indicators (KPI). These KPIs will be transferred into business as usual after the programme closes and will be the subject of regular reports to the MPS Management Board.

Ailsa Beaton, MPS director of information, commented:

'C3i was an enormously complex programme, with a very simple overall objective: to ensure we could continue to provide an excellent police response service to the people of London. The programme offers a huge range of benefits to the organisation, from better management information to scalable and flexible technologies. Because of that, we can offer the public a robust and resilient response police service based on a more effective use of resources. The C3i Programme was a means to an end, but it was also the start of a new way of doing business. The organisation can use the Benefits Framework to realise the full range of potential offered by the new technology, and – over the coming years – explore the opportunities for further exploitation of the additional capacity.'

OGC REVIEWS

The OGC Gateway Process is an independent peer review which provides guidance to sponsors and programme teams on how best to ensure that their programmes and projects are successful. The gateway reviews take place during the programme as follows:

Gateway 0	Strategic Assessment
Gateway 1	Business Justification
Gateway 2	Procurement Strategy
Gateway 3	Investment Decision
Gateway 4	Readiness for Service
Gateway 5	Benefits Evaluation

C3i was one of the first such public sector programmes to reach the OGC's Gateway 5 review, and was commended by the review team for both its management and its delivery.

The MPS C3i case highlights the importance of stakeholder management and governance.

STAKEHOLDER MANAGEMENT

For an organisation to be successful in IT-enabled business change it needs strong governance, management and execution. Governance provides an accountability framework to ensure effective business alignment and management of risk. This requires clarity of the roles of the stakeholders, who are defined as anyone who holds a 'stake' or interest in the change. The stakeholder concept is important in the IT-enabled business change field, and the tag of stakeholder applies to many of those who were targeted as the audience for this book in the *Introduction* chapter.

Key internal stakeholder roles include sponsor, business analyst, programme manager, business change manager and business actor. As highlighted previously, there are many other stakeholders such as the IT specialists involved in planning and delivery plus the senior executives who are committed to improving the organisational capability in IT-enabled business change. There are also many external stakeholders to be considered including government, customers, suppliers, IS consultants, trade unions and competitors. The following section will explore these roles in more detail.

Stakeholder management is the process of analysing and engaging with both internal and external stakeholders. By considering their relative power and interests, stakeholders can be categorised and then represented by the quadrants within a 2 × 2 grid. The grid helps to analyse the position of stakeholders in order to highlight what action needs to be taken to manage their engagement and their expectations. There are many variations in the contents of the grid and Figure 2.2 highlights just two of the typical issues.

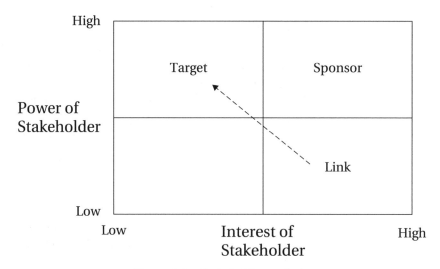

FIGURE 2.2   *Stakeholder analysis*

Figure 2.2 shows the most important stakeholder, the sponsor, who must be in the high power and high interest quadrant. If the sponsor is not clearly identified or not in this quadrant there is a high risk regarding buy-in from others to the IT-enabled business change. You may find that a key executive whom you wish to actively engage is in the high power and low interest quadrant and therefore needs to increase their interest level. One way of making a connection is through another stakeholder. The obvious one is the sponsor but there may be no existing relationship between them. Another option is to identify a stakeholder with low power but high interest who is an influencer of the target stakeholder. This process of analysing the relationships within a community or organisation is known as social network analysis.

There is another dimension that you will need to consider and that is whether the stakeholder supports or opposes the change. If a stakeholder has high power but low interest it is particularly important to ensure that they are not against the change. In most organisations you will need to assess the positions of the finance and human resource directors, given their influence over money and people decisions.

Stakeholders and their positioning often evolve throughout the IT-enabled business change life cycle. Hence the position of each stakeholder group should be evaluated at different stages. Before a decision is made on whether to develop or buy an IT solution there will be little focus on the supplier as a stakeholder. After the decision to buy, the supplier becomes a critical stakeholder in ensuring a workable solution.

Similarly, at the alignment stage, many of the executives and senior managers will want to be involved to understand how the proposed business change impacts their part of the organisation. Once this is clear those not directly involved in the change will be less interested until the implementation stage, when their staff members are impacted by changes taking place elsewhere. For example, the sales director decides that proposed automation of the warehouse is beneficial and adopts a hands-off approach until the implementation causes delivery problems that adversely impact customers and sales revenue.

It is also the case that some significant organisation changes take place over a long period. During this time the business outlook can deteriorate and this can affect how senior executives view a proposal. For example, the director of finance may support the change when profits in the organisation are high but then want to see much more detail behind the financial benefits if external cost pressures arise.

The key message is to adopt a structured approach to understanding who are the key stakeholders, re-evaluate their position over time and tailor the engagement approach according to this positioning.

EXERCISE

Take a situation at work or at home where a key decision needs to be made and which involves a number of stakeholders. It may be an organisation project or deciding on a family event such as whether and where to go on holiday. Identify the stakeholders, map them onto the stakeholder grid and decide how you will engage them.

ROLES AND RESPONSIBILITIES OF KEY STAKEHOLDERS

This section builds on the audience perspectives of the first chapter and the stakeholder view of the previous section. The focus is primarily on the key stakeholder roles of IT-enabled business change with supplementary information on related stakeholder roles. These key roles are as follows:

(i) Sponsor – this role oversees the change and the delivery of the benefits.

(ii) Business analysts – these ensure a business-driven approach to the change.

(iii) Programme manager – this role plans and ensures delivery of the change.

(iv) Business change manager – this role manages the change in the business.

(v) Business actors – these provide knowledge of key business areas.

Sponsor

The sponsor role is a critical one in IT-enabled change. This is the person who has commissioned the project or to whom the organisation has entrusted the responsibility for delivering the business benefits. It will be the sponsor who works with the sponsoring group to make funds and other resources available for the project and who will be asked to confirm that the deliverables have been met at the end of the change.

The sponsoring group represents the needs and interests of the organisation as a whole, with the sponsor acting on behalf of this group and accountable for the delivery of the benefits. It is important to have people in this group that are committed both to making the change and to realising the benefits. The sponsoring group may be the top management team of an organisation or result from a specially formed steering group.

The importance and influence of the sponsor is often underestimated. This is highlighted by research done on the factors that drive successful IT-enabled change and in particular the role of the business sponsor (Manwani 2007). The research commenced with a broad review of the literature, which was used as a foundation to test and develop insights with focus groups of experienced practitioners. One overall conclusion was that reported failures are not just a consequence of the technology since problems are generally associated with any large-scale business change.

The research identified that the biggest challenge for the sponsor is to combine the dual roles of stewardship and leadership. Stewardship ensures that the business case is sound and that funds and resources are available and appropriately used. Leadership is about engaging with stakeholders and creating a persuasive, compelling vision. The more complex and pervasive the change, the more critical is the sponsor's role. However, the skills required of a sponsor are often not well understood by the organisation nor often by the holder of the role. Most of the advice on IT-enabled change tends to stress the methodological approach, which is a necessary foundation but not sufficient for success. Little guidance is available on the behavioural leadership traits that are vital for the sponsor to demonstrate and exercise in a context of complexity and uncertainty.

Why is the focus on the sponsor role so critical in complex change given that increasingly IT project and programme managers are becoming more professional and more successful? Partly it is a question of maturity. Many project managers have several projects to their credit where they have been able to navigate and balance scope, time and cost in a well-bounded business area with proven technology. Experienced programme managers are scarcer although many have now understood the methodological complexity of managing interdependent projects. Where they need support is in the political dimension of a programme. Yet relatively few change sponsors have taken on multiple initiatives and seen the full consequences of their decisions. See for example the data below on Senior Responsible Owners arising from a survey by the National Audit Office. There are different terms used for the sponsor and the term Senior Responsible Owner (SRO) is one that is used in the UK Government arena.

SENIOR RESPONSIBLE OWNER SURVEY

In the UK public sector Senior Responsible Owner is the title given to a sponsor of major IT change programmes. Every major IT change programme or project is expected to have an SRO (usually a senior civil servant) to take overall responsibility for making sure that the programme meets its objectives and delivers the projected benefits. The SRO key tasks include developing the business case and monitoring the progress and the risks to delivery, which involves strong liaison with key stakeholders in the organisation.

A survey was conducted in 2006 to establish the views of 40 SROs on the results and processes of mission critical and high risk IT-enabled business change programmes being done across central government in 2006.

(Continued)

(Continued)

> Over 50% of the sample audience were undertaking their first assignment as an SRO. Forty-five per cent of the SROs spent one day or less a week in this role. Just over 50% of the SROs met with the CIO/IT director either weekly or monthly to review the project or programme.
>
> Source: National Audit Office[3]

POINT TO PONDER

Reflect on the survey results and consider if the time spent and level of support for SROs is about right. What are the factors that should influence the time spent on this role?

The role of sponsors varies at different stages of the change. It is harder to define the scope of the change at the alignment stage of an IT-enabled business change than it is in later stages. The sponsor needs to focus more on innovation than management during this stage. In this 'fuzzy' front-end there is a great deal of ambiguity with diverse aims from multiple stakeholders in different parts of the business. Reconciling these perspectives into a clear scope and mandate for a programme is a challenge even for the most skilled of sponsors.

During the business improvement and design stages there is a need to generate a range of options that are aligned to the business strategy. These can be evaluated using risk/reward scenarios and the sponsor needs to take a key role in facilitating this process with senior colleagues in the organisation. In terms of leadership, there is a need for passion, decisiveness and the political ability to form alliances.

Finally in the implementation and benefits stages the emphasis needs to be on achieving the business outcome. The sponsor should ensure that resources are appropriately dedicated as much to the business change as they are to the IT solution. It is important to avoid complacency – when things are going well, sponsors should concentrate much of their energy on potential risks. One way of reducing risk is to simplify processes, at least as much as is possible, and then recognise that the need is to cope with the resulting complexity.

The political skills of the sponsor (using this term in a positive sense) come very much into play in the definition of success. This has many forms with personal as well as organisational ambitions changing over time. Being able to articulate the benefits is a key skill required by a sponsor. Further, when success comes it is important to celebrate it and recognise that on a tough and long journey that may need to happen more than once.

In summary, for organisations undertaking transformational change the landscape for sponsors is complex and ambiguous. Success depends upon their leadership ability to balance the vested interests of different players, as well as establishing credibility in a stewardship role.

Business analyst

The business analyst role is fundamental in delivering successful IT-enabled business change. A definition of this role follows from the OGC[4]:

> 'Business analysts are responsible for identifying and documenting the functional and non-functional requirements for meeting business need. They should have a good understanding of the business area and be able to identify opportunities for effective use of IT.'

This role may be performed by an internal or external consultant. They are the team member in a development group or programme who is mainly responsible for gathering, analysing, specifying and validating the IT-enabled business change requirements. Where the requirements result in the development, customisation or procurement of IT systems the analyst needs to act as a 'bridge' between the business stakeholders and the systems developers and to be able to communicate with both these parties (Paul and Yeates 2006).

There are some specific responsibilities that are normally within the job description of a business analyst. These include dealing with change requests from business users who have improvement suggestions or problems with the existing systems. This is one way of gathering requirements. Alternatively the business analyst may be a member of a change programme team, in which case the requirements will be generated by goals set by the senior management of an organisation. Even in this latter case there are likely to be change requests to deal with as the programme evolves. Whichever route is taken, the business analyst has a key part to play in the front-end definition of a business solution.

There is also an important activity later in the IT-enabled business change life cycle, namely testing the solution before it is installed in a live environment. The business analyst will be involved in the identification of test scenarios that correspond to the IT-enabled business change requirements identified in the earlier phase. This is a vital input to the acceptance of the business solution by the operational users.

Acceptance of the solution is facilitated by effective communications. These include informing and working with the business managers on how the new solution is likely to impact the organisation. Business analysts require the knowledge of how the business processes are designed to operate and the appropriate stakeholder management skills to facilitate improvements.

Another activity required before the go-live stage of a new solution is the training of the operational users, sometimes called 'end-user training'. The business analyst with the knowledge of how the system is designed to operate is well-placed to plan the training approach. Following implementation the business analyst is likely to be involved in reviewing how well the system is working and whether the benefits are being realised.

In summary, while business analysts have a key role across the whole IT-enabled business change life cycle, they have a particularly strong focus in the front-end and back-end stages of the change programme.

Programme management

The programme and project managers take direct responsibility for the management of the IT-enabled change. There is much debate about the difference between a project and a programme and hence the roles of the people managing these changes.

First there is a need to distinguish between business operations and business change. Many tasks require management as part of normal business operations and these activities and actions are not classified as projects. However, any significant organisation change should be managed as a project or programme. It is an organisational decision to define the parameters for this being viewed as significant in terms of size, complexity, risk and impact.

There are many definitions of a project including the following one from PRINCE2® (Projects In a Controlled Environment)[5], which highlights the management environment for the change and the delivered business products: 'A management environment that is created for the purpose of delivering one or more business products according to a specified Business Case.'

There is another definition which highlights that a project needs to be managed across the three parameters of specification, time and cost. It highlights the boundaries of a project: 'A project delivers a defined scope within agreed cost and time budgets.'

A broader definition of a project follows; this is one that focuses more on a framework and outcomes than outputs and can more readily be applied to a business change project: 'It is an organisation structure through which a business change is implemented that is aligned to a strategic goal.'

A programme has an additional characteristic in that it encompasses a set of interdependent projects. This results in a further layer of complexity. A programme can be defined as follows: 'A change programme delivers an improved strategic capability through a set of interdependent projects.'

Following on from these definitions the management activity for projects and programmes can be described as follows: 'Project and programme management encompass the activities of defining, planning, controlling and completing projects and programmes.'

The programme manager is the person who is responsible for planning, monitoring and controlling the suite of projects that will deliver the business changes. The key element of this role is to ensure that all of the projects are co-ordinated and any dependencies between the projects are identified and managed.

In managing a project experienced managers realise that it is important to consider both the 'hard' and the 'soft' factors. It is one of the biggest challenges in a project to get this balance right. Examples of these are shown below.

Hard factors:

- scope;
- methodology;
- tools;
- organisation and technical risk;
- training.

Soft factors:

- leadership;
- team;
- roles and culture;
- communication and behavioural risk;
- participation and commitment.

The hard factors are those that are often covered in a process-based course for new project managers. This training typically demonstrates how project managers can use methodologies to create a plan that deals with scope, time and risk. It will identify tools such as Gantt charts and risk registers to support these plans. Where the focus is on people, it tends to be on well-defined areas such as the need to train staff in using a new system.

The soft factors are those that are required in any management role, tailored to a project context. There is a need to build and lead a team, ensuring that the roles are clearly defined and appropriate to the organisational culture. Effective communication is vital in building participation and commitment to the team and business goals.

It is not easy to acquire both the hard and soft sets of skills. Where there is a programme consisting of multiple interdependent projects, the programme manager will need to demonstrate the people skills and be prepared if necessary to delegate some of the process activities to the project managers or the programme office. A project manager in a large project will benefit from having a project office that can administer and follow-up on project plans. Without this capability, the risk is that the project manager will be overburdened at the task level and therefore unable to spend sufficient time interacting with stakeholders.

Business change manager

The business change manager role has been described in detail by the OGC. Its focus is primarily on the changes in the business process and the resulting benefits. The holder of this role is responsible, on behalf of the sponsor or SRO, for defining the benefits, assessing progress towards realisation and achieving measured improvements. Hence the business change manager role is a key link between programme management and business operations. Business change managers require a detailed knowledge and experience of the business organisation including the management structures, governance and culture. They need specific knowledge of the business area that is being changed and the skills to communicate the programme vision and benefits to staff at all levels of the organisation.

In some organisations there is a specialist business change management function. This group helps to define new initiatives and works with the business functions on change programmes. There may be project management and business analyst roles within this group. The business change function will liaise with the IT department on IT-enabled business change projects.

Business actor

The business actor role represents all of the people who carry out the work of the business areas represented by the change. For example in a company-wide change this may include staff from different business functions such as marketing, sales, customer services, finance and human resources. Where there are large numbers of people in these areas, a team of selected people may be set up to represent each of the groups. The business actor is sometimes called a 'super user' to reflect their knowledge of the area. As well as providing knowledge in the early part of the change programme, they may also be asked to participate in designing and executing the testing of the business process scenarios.

These business actors are critical to the success of an IT-enabled change programme. Historically many projects were IT-driven partly due to the technical complexity of creating a new system. Business users were expected to implement what was provided to them, sometimes with very limited training due to the inevitable time pressures at the end of a project. Many organisations now recognise that a strong business involvement is needed throughout the change and that there are different types and levels of expertise required. One challenge that remains is allocating sufficient time for the business activities since these are often not as visible from a budgeting and solutions viewpoint as the delivery and testing of a new system.

IT specialist roles

In addition to the key IT roles in IT-enabled change there are specialist IT and information delivery roles that will be required in the project, depending on the scope of the change. The IT roles that are required at the front-end of a programme are those that help to set the strategic requirements into an overall context and to scope the IT contribution to the improvement. Relevant roles may include strategic planning, architecture and IT innovation.

The strategic planning role will help in aligning the business and IT strategies while the innovation role will identify specific opportunities arising from IT, with the exploitation of the internet being a prime example in recent years. The architect looks to the future while considering how systems and technologies can evolve from their current position to the future state. In the business change design stage the architect has a key role to play in defining the key components of the proposed solution.

The development of the system in an IT-enabled change programme is a key step that requires specialist skills throughout the systems development life cycle covering systems analysis, systems design, systems build, systems testing and systems implementation.

The systems management role should have a say in how this part of a major programme is to be managed through to the implementation of the business change. One of the key responsibilities will be to ensure that the necessary resources are allocated to the systems activities. Once the system is implemented, it is critical that it works according to the agreed service level so as not to risk the target benefits. If the response times for an ordering system on the internet are too long, for example, customers are likely to go elsewhere.

Hence service level management is a key role that will liaise with the roles responsible for creating the IT infrastructure. Depending on the nature of the IT-enabled change programme there may be many other specialist roles required, such as information security and data analysis. For a comprehensive list of the IT skills that provide an insight into the potential roles there is a website providing a Skills Framework for the Information Age (SFIA)[6]. Business change skills from SFIA are described later in the book.

SUMMARY

This overview of IT-enabled business change has stressed the importance of understanding the different stages in the IT-enabled business change life cycle and appointing people to the key roles in making this change effective. The sponsor provides leadership and governance for the change. A key role is that of the business analyst, who has the responsibility for analysing business situations, documenting resulting requirements and identifying options for improving business systems by bridging the needs of the business with the use of IT. The delivery is led by the programme or project manager. These roles work closely with the business change managers, who oversee changes in the user work processes with the support of business actors, who are those individuals who have an interest in, or may be affected by, the business change project.

Other roles are involved in IT-enabled change. IT roles include architects, designers and developers of the system. The people supporting and growing organisational capability include the CIO, who facilitates creation of the overall environment for business change. Everyone working on an IT-enabled change programme needs awareness of the big picture. The rationale for creating a new book is so that most people in an organisation can be provided with a degree of knowledge to understand how they contribute to the successful implementation of change. The following chapters will consider what knowledge is required at each stage of the IT-enabled change life cycle.

TOPICS: LIFE CYCLE OVERVIEW

This chapter provides a view of IT-enabled business change that covers the process as well as studying the key stakeholders and their role within the process. It has introduced the concept of the business change life cycle. The chapter covers:

- The definition of the term 'IT-enabled business change'.
- IT as a driver for business improvement.
- IT as a core competence within the organisation.
- The business change life cycle.
- The stages in the business change life cycle.
- The definition of the term 'stakeholder'.
- The range of stakeholder groups.
- The roles and responsibilities of key stakeholders:
  - sponsor;
  - business analyst;
  - programme manager;
  - business change manager;
  - business actor.

SAMPLE QUESTIONS

Question 1

IT-enabled business change is concerned with:

(a) making business changes to match the capabilities of the purchased software packages;
(b) ensuring that all functions within the organisation use IT;
(c) using new technology developments as quickly as possible;
(d) improving business performance through the application of IT.

Discussion

The focus of the first three possible answers is more on the IT than the business change. In the last response, the focus is on changing business performance enabled by IT.

Question 2

Which of the following ideally represents the role of technology in an IT enabled enterprise?

(a) It is an enabler for achieving the strategy of an organisation.
(b) It is one of the external drivers of business strategy.
(c) It is both a driver and an enabler of business strategy.
(d) It is neither a driver nor an enabler of business strategy.

Discussion

Where an enterprise depends on IT, the ideal state is that technology opportunities will be taken to drive the business strategy and IT is an enabler for the strategy to be implemented.

Question 3

Which of the following provides the most complete definition of a stakeholder?

(a) Someone who has an interest in the business change project.
(b) A competitor organisation.
(c) An individual member of staff who will use the new IT system.
(d) Anyone who holds a senior management position in the organisation.

Discussion

You will see from the *Glossary* that a stakeholder is defined as someone with an interest in the change. Categories may include: customers, employees, managers, partners, regulators, owners, suppliers and contractors.

While the roles in the other answers may in certain circumstances be a stakeholder, this is not necessarily the case.

Question 4

Which of the following roles has the responsibility for planning a business change project?

  (a) Programme manager.
  (b) Business analyst.
  (c) Management consultant.
  (d) Business actor.

Discussion

The business analyst and actors are key roles in **executing** a business change project. A management consultant may be hired to support the programme manager but it is the latter who has the overall responsibility.

Question 5

What is the primary role of a business sponsor in an IT-enabled change programme?

  (a) To manage the delivery of the outputs against the plan.
  (b) To appoint the teams including selection of suppliers.
  (c) To ensure that customers understand the change programme.
  (d) To be accountable for the outcomes.

Discussion

The business sponsor is not directly responsible for managing the execution of elements of the programme. These are assigned to other roles such as the programme manager and business change manager. Sponsors are accountable for the outcomes of the change programme such as ensuring that targeted benefits are assured.

Question 6

A business actor must be able to:

  (a) manage the achievement of the business case;
  (b) analyse and model business requirements;
  (c) represent the interests of the entire group of business users;
  (d) provide information about the business domain.

Discussion

A business actor does not have a development responsibility for the programme. Their role is to support the programme, for example by providing relevant information about a specific part of their domain.

Question 7

The senior responsible owner/project owner (SRO/PO) is the individual responsible for ensuring that a project or programme of change meets its objectives and delivers the projected benefits. Which of the following two managerial roles are accountable to the SRO/PO?

(a) Programme manager and business change manager.
(b) Business sponsor and project manager.
(c) Programme manager and programme office manager.
(d) IT manager and business change manager.

Discussion

Senior responsible owner and project owner are terms used, particularly in UK Government, to describe the role of the sponsor. In this structure the person responsible for delivering the programme overall (programme manager) and the person responsible for ensuring readiness for change (business change manager) both report to the SRO.

3 Business and IT Alignment

Business IT alignment is not a one-off task. It requires an ongoing focus and engagement with key stakeholders.

Phil Ives, Head of Information Services, Yell

INTRODUCING ALIGNMENT

Organisations need to review and align with the environment within which their business operates. This requires strategic thinking and approaches to align internal capability to external demands. In pursuit of this goal, there are many approaches to developing strategy supported by frameworks covering a scope such as competitive advantage or core competencies. The former starts with an analysis of the external environment, in particular the industry in which the organisation operates. In contrast, the core competencies approach focuses initially on the internal capabilities of the organisation. Whichever is the starting point for the strategic development, organisations need to understand the external drivers and opportunities and how these match to existing and desired internal capabilities.

Similarly, it is important to ensure that there is a fit between the business and IT directions of the organisation. The business goals need to be considered with regard to the possibilities offered by IT and the use of IT must be aligned to the business goals. Business and IT alignment is the process of ensuring that the investments in information technology are matched to the strategic goals of the business. These two dimensions of alignment are represented in Figure 3.1.

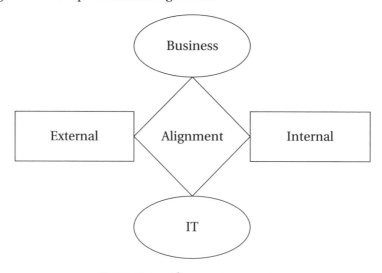

FIGURE 3.1 *Alignment perspectives*

This chapter introduces a range of techniques to support alignment. Many are covered in business management courses and are often applied in large organisations. While these often provide a valuable guide, frameworks should not be regarded as an alternative to strategic thinking.

The first part of this chapter focuses on the external and internal elements of business alignment using an overarching framework. It then reviews how environment and industry perspectives are matched with internal goals and culture. Widely used models are introduced in support of these perspectives.

The second part of the chapter explores many facets of business and IT alignment. This starts with the positive and negative impacts of IT. To deal with these impacts a proactive and forward-thinking approach is required, which is provided through the next topic of IT governance and architecture. This is followed by the management of IT-enabled business change risks, which is one of the key elements of effective governance and completed by highlighting the need for senior management commitment. The final part covers outsourcing, building on both the first and second parts since it requires a strategic external–internal perspective as well as strong business IT alignment.

EXTERNAL AND INTERNAL BUSINESS ENVIRONMENT

SWOT analysis is a relatively simple but powerful model which considers both the external and internal perspectives. SWOT stands for:

S   Strengths;
W   Weaknesses;
O   Opportunities;
T   Threats.

TOWS represents these terms in reverse order. The strengths and weaknesses relate to the organisation itself while the threats and opportunities arise from an external analysis. Strengths and weaknesses should be considered in relation to competitors or alternative providers of the organisation's products and services. It is useful to obtain a customer's perspective as well as an internal evaluation to ensure an objective viewpoint.

As shown in Figure 3.2 there is an interaction between the internal and external perspectives. Identifying the strengths will lead to understanding related potential opportunities. For example, a consumer products organisation that is good at building relationships with major customers will benefit from an external scenario where consolidation is taking place in the market sector due to large retailers acquiring smaller ones.

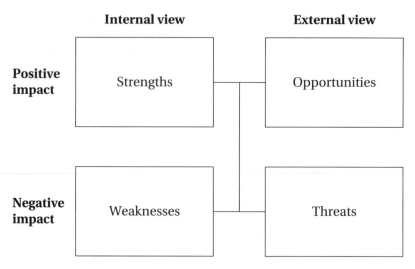

FIGURE 3.2   *SWOT analysis*

POINT TO PONDER

Review the organisation you work for or select one that you can research. Identify the strengths, weaknesses, threats and opportunities. Where does IT fit in each of these categories?

You may also find it useful to conduct a SWOT analysis on yourself in relation to your current or desired job.

External Influences

External influences may be expressed by taking a broad look at the environment to understand which trends might have a major impact on the organisation. One of the most common tools to help identify the key external drivers or factors is labelled by the acronym PEST:

Political – the current and potential influences from political pressures.

Economic – the local, national, regional and world economy impact.

Sociological – the ways in which changes in society affect the organisation.

Technological – the effect of new and emerging technology.

PESTLE is an extension of the original acronym, PEST, to include two additional factors:

Legal – the effect of national, regional and world legislation.

Environmental – the local, national, regional and world environmental issues.

These broad factors are likely to impact most organisations operating in a particular industry. For example, a regulation on food standards related to labelling is likely to affect all the supermarket retailers. In Europe, the regional perspective is a strong one with the influence of the European Community.

Industry analysis and organisation strategy

We need to understand how organisations interact with each other within a particular industry or sector. This will involve engagement with external stakeholders such as customers, suppliers and competitors. Many strategic models relate to the analysis of competitive advantage with three of the most widely known being those developed by Michael Porter[7].

The first strategic model covers the generic strategies and involves a decision made by an organisation to choose between being a low-cost producer, competing through strong product or service differentiation, or focusing on a particular segment of the market with one of these two strategies. Figure 3.3 depicts Porter's three generic strategies.

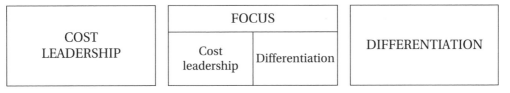

FIGURE 3.3   *Generic strategies*

As with any strategic choice, deciding to invest in one area reduces the resources available to another area. A luxury product will aim for a strong brand to command a high price whereas a commodity product will usually need to compete on price. Certain industries, such as cosmetics, are more geared to luxury goods and others, such as fuel, to commodities. However, even within these overall categories there is scope for different competitive strategies.

> **POINT TO PONDER**
>
> *One illustration of a market which demonstrates different positions is the automotive industry. Consider the perceptions of automotive brands such as Ford, Ferrari, Mercedes and Skoda. Where do they fit in terms of competitive positioning and to what extent has this shifted over time?*

A second strategic tool supports the analysis of the forces in the industry. Porter identified five main forces. The first four forces also influence the fifth force:

(i)   the barriers and threats of new entrants;

(ii) the availability and threats of substitute products;

(iii) the bargaining power of buyers;

(iv) the bargaining power of suppliers;

(v)   the level of competitive rivalry among existing competitors.

There are many elements in each of these forces. For example, the bargaining power will depend on the number of buyers, since a small number concentrates the power. Before setting its own strategy an organisation needs to understand the competitive forces since this will to some extent shape the industry, limit the level of profitability and influence its options. There is some debate about how applicable the five forces model is in the public sector since profitability is not a key driver. (Note: Porter produced an update on the five forces model published in the *Harvard Business Review* in January 2008.)

POINT TO PONDER

Consider the oil industry and assess how easy or difficult it is for a new company to enter the market.

Finally, one of the most widely used tools for understanding how an organisation within an industry adds value is the value chain. It is most obviously applied to analysing companies that manufacture and sell products; however, it can also be applied to a range of organisations in other industries including the service and public sectors. The generic value chain illustrates how value is directly added by primary activities such as inbound logistics, operations, outbound logistics, marketing/sales and service, which directly contribute to a financial margin being earned in the marketplace. Secondary activities in the generic value chain are procurement, accounting, human resources and technology and these are important enablers for effective operation of these primary activities.

In Figure 3.4, which is an adaptation of Porter's generic value chain, simplified terms are used to denote the primary activities (buy, make, deliver, sell, service) and the secondary activities (source, report, employ, compute). These terms are not standard ones and are shown only to illustrate that it is feasible to tailor the generic activities for an organisation.

The value chain is a particularly useful tool for assessing the linkages between different activities and how well information supports these linkages. As indicated in Figure 3.4 there is a need to share information between different functions in order to operate key business processes that allow an organisation to buy, make and sell the right number of products. Hence, the value chain can be used to identify information flows and gaps between related primary activities or between primary and secondary activities.

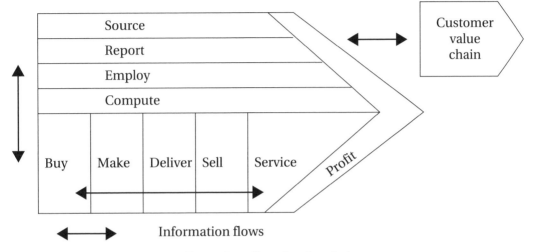

FIGURE 3.4 *Sample value chain*

Value chains can also be combined between organisations in an industry to create a value system. This provides a useful tool to analyse the information flows and gaps between these organisations. This is illustrated above with an information flow to a customer value chain.

Organisation capability

Competitive advantage approaches start with an analysis of the external factors whereas the core competences approach (Hamel and Prahalad 1990) starts with an understanding of the organisation's capabilities. A core competency is a business capability that provides perceived benefits to the customer, is difficult for competitors to imitate and contributes to many products or markets. The existence of these capabilities can be determined by asking questions such as: does the organisation have patented designs, a well-regarded brand and talented people?

POINT TO PONDER

The Virgin brand is applied to different products such as an airline, railway and financial services. To what extent does brand management need to be a core competence in Virgin?

The organisation will generally be in a good position if its identified strengths from the SWOT analysis are also supportive of its intended core competencies. At the same time it should assess how important these strengths are to the organisation in relation to the external scenarios. For example, a travel consultancy may wish to develop a competency in creating luxury holidays, and over time its range of products may become a strength. However, a major downturn in the market due to an economic recession may reduce this advantage and have a negative impact on profitability.

Internally it is advantageous to align the business goals at the different levels of the organisation. MOST is a tool to support this type of analysis:

M   Mission;
O   Objectives;
S   Strategy;
T   Tactics.

The **mission** of an organisation defines why it exists in terms of its core activities, customers and products. It represents the fundamental purpose of an organisation. Many large organisations publish their missions on their websites.

EXERCISE

Look for different missions by entering 'mission statement' with the name of a well-known organisation through a search engine such as Google. What do they have in common? How are they different?

The **objectives** will define top-level goals, ideally with quantified outcomes within a given time period. These will be consistent with the organisation mission and external environment. For example the objective might be to increase revenue by 10% in the next two years. There will be a range of **strategic options** to achieve the objectives. For example, the growth in revenue may come from existing or new customers. Specific **tactics** can be employed that align with these strategies, such as creating consumer promotions to stimulate demand for products.

There is an extension of the MOST model to VMOST, where V represents the **vision** of an organisation that describes where it sees itself in the future. The vision should convey the sense of a journey and this distinguishes it from the underlying mission of an organisation.

The VMOST model provides a structured approach to identify both strategic and tactical approaches to meet the objectives of an organisation. What it does not explicitly do is to consider the target values and culture.

YELL GROUP

'Yell is a leading international directories business operating in the classified advertising market in the United Kingdom, United States, Spain and Latin America. Yell creates value by putting buyers in touch with sellers through an integrated portfolio of simple to use, cost-effective advertising products available in print, online and over the phone.'

'We aim to be the best business information bridge between buyers and sellers, regardless of channel, time or location. Yell seeks to understand, anticipate and meet the changing demands of advertisers and users and to take advantage of new technologies and communication methods in the development of world-class products and services.'

Consider how these statements, sourced from the Yell website, fit into a VMOST model.

Understanding culture

Culture is sometimes simply referred to as 'the way things get done around here' (Deal and Kennedy 1982). It is often a key enabler or inhibitor of productive outputs in an organisation. By understanding the culture of your target environment for change you can start to identify the potential resistance and how you might adopt different strategies to address these concerns and issues. There are many different cultural frameworks. Two widely used models are Handy's organisational culture types and Hofstede's international culture dimensions.

Handy (1993) identifies four types of organisational culture:

- Power culture is one where power is centralised in the top executives of the organisation.
- Role culture is a bureaucracy with highly structured, well-documented procedures.
- Task culture emphasises getting things done through empowerment, flexibility and teams.
- Person culture is focused around the individuals, who may be connected through a common set of strong values.

The culture should fit the nature of an organisation. A professional services people-orientated business which is operating in a high business change environment is less likely to benefit from a bureaucratic role culture than a health and safety organisation. Likewise, it is useful to think about how to implement change given the culture. Imposing a change 'top-down' from the chief executive with no consultation with employees is unlikely to work well in a person culture.

POINT TO PONDER

What is the culture in your organisation? Is there a strong fit between what is communicated as the values of the organisation and the way it works in practice?

The culture of a multinational organisation will be impacted to some extent by the national culture of the head office. Additionally, if change is going to be implemented in a country, the national culture of the subsidiary will be relevant. There may be challenges if the culture of the head office and the subsidiary are very different. For this, we need to apply an international cultural diagnostic such as that provided by Hofstede.

Hofstede (2001) researched the culture of different nations, initially identifying four dimensions and later adding a fifth. These dimensions are measured on a spectrum from high to low:

- High power distance is one where members expect that power is distributed unequally and are less likely to question the person at the top.
- High individualism is a society in which the ties between individuals are loose in which people are expected to look after themselves and their family. The opposite is collectivism.
- High masculinity is a society where values such as assertiveness and competitiveness are more prevalent and where women are less likely to be treated as equals. The opposite is femininity.
- High uncertainty avoidance occurs where a society has a low tolerance for uncertainty and ambiguity. The opposite is low uncertainty avoidance and people in this type of culture are more comfortable with ambiguity.
- Long-term orientation versus short-term orientation is a fifth dimension added later where long-term orientation derives from values such as perseverance.

There are logical connections between the two cultural models. We can postulate that a society with low power distance is one where members of the head office of the organisation feel more able to question their managers and it is less likely that this will be a power culture organisation.

AN EXAMPLE OF INTERNATIONAL BUSINESS CHANGE

A major international appliance manufacturer had grown as a result of over 100 acquisitions. It needed an operating model to link multiple international factories to national sales companies in order to be

(Continued)

(Continued)

more market responsive. At the same time, the growth of international retailers required a tailored approach to each key account, which was a different operating model. Further complexity existed due to the growth of the internet and the potential to deal directly with consumers resulting in a third potential operating model.

Initially the European CEO favoured the key account approach as a way of driving change. However, the organisation culture was neither consistent nor a power culture – a result of many countries being represented in the European structure and the nature of the head office national culture. The Head Office was in Sweden and staff appeared comfortable with uncertainty; however, this was not the case in all the subsidiaries, for example in Germany.

The CEO and CIO reviewed the different options and eventually realised that tailored strategies were needed to respond to the three operating models with significantly varying IT systems. They agreed on a combination of methodologies in order to build robust systems, pilots and prototypes for the three operating models at the same time. This meant that certainty was a feature of the core operating model specification yet the pilot and prototypes could be built as flexible models in a more uncertain environment.

The lesson from this case is the need to define operating models based around the customer needs. The customer of the factory in the first model was the sales company, in the second model the key account and in the third model the consumer. It was vital that the CEO and CIO were both involved in the design of the operating models given the major business and IT implications. Further, they needed to take into account the cultural aspects in defining the best implementation approach.

IMPACT OF IT

In some cases, IT will be one of the core competencies of an organisation. This is more likely to be the case in an industry where IT directly supports the product or the relationship of the organisation with the customer. If this support is provided effectively, the IT capability can be regarded as a strength. However, it is also possible that IT is a weakness in that the installed base of systems, sometimes called legacy systems, may be a barrier to change. This will be the case if the organisation needs to transform its business processes and rules but the systems modifications take so long that there is a negative impact on external and internal stakeholders.

IT may also be a source of an opportunity for example with the growth of the internet as a trading tool. An organisation that has previously traded only through shops may be able to use the internet to reach a wider audience. There may also be an associated threat, for example the organisation may be open to virus and IT security attacks because of operating as an online business.

It can be argued that IT has two broad beneficial impacts on an organisation, with, however, potential negative consequences if these are not designed and executed appropriately. As we have seen with earlier examples, the impact can be of the order of millions of pounds and in a few cases this can make the difference between the survival and failure of the organisation.

IT and business operations

The first positive impact of IT is the support of the business operations, represented for example by the activities in the value chain. Each function, such as sales, purchasing and finance, will follow a series of steps to carry out the basic transactions, such as taking and fulfilling orders. Many of these steps can be automated through IT, such as sending an order from one part of the organisation to another, executing business rules such as credit checks and printing documents such as invoices.

If the IT applications do not work effectively the related business operations will almost certainly cost more or take longer to reach an acceptable outcome. For example, if an incorrect price is entered into the system the invoice for the products will have the wrong total. When the customer realises this they will make a complaint that will involve customer services as the interface and the finance group to raise a credit note and make the accounting adjustments. If a pricing error affects a large number of customers one inaccurate entry will have a large negative impact.

There is also a potential negative impact from a failure of the IT service, for example computer downtime due to a hardware failure. In the past such a failure in IT operations might have taken some time to be realised at the customer interface, if at all. With the growth of the internet, many more businesses are conducting operations with their customers in real-time and these online transactions are very visibly affected by any breakdown in IT services.

IT and business information

The second impact arises from the use of IT to gather, consolidate and present meaningful information to the organisation to support key decisions. If the information does not go to the right person at the right time, this may lead to a missed opportunity or poor decision. One of the challenges is to extract the data such as orders from the operational systems and group it by customer or product so that decisions can be made. However, calculations such as customer profitability are not at all straightforward and organisations can end up putting resources into the wrong areas due to misleading information.

Decisions are often made on imperfect information such as future customer buying patterns. A purchasing manager typically needs to take a decision on how much material to buy in advance of receiving a firm order from a customer. How does this manager make the right decision to have enough material but not so much that the organisation has money tied up in stock that may potentially never be required? An IT system can support the decision by collecting historic information about sales patterns combined with forecasts of sales in order to predict likely material usage and propose order quantities.

A key design factor in an information system is how much scope there is for a user to take a decision contrary to that proposed by the system. This will be partly dependent on how much of the information is available within the system. For example, there should be the opportunity for a purchasing manager to use additional knowledge not contained within the IT system, such as a risk of worldwide shortages, to override the recommended figures.

In the past, much of the information that was provided to managers was structured data such as the quantitative monthly sales data. Increasingly IT systems are being used to collect and help exploit unstructured data such as the knowledge of customers acquired by the sales force through building relationships.

> **POINT TO PONDER**
>
> *What are the positive and negative impacts of IT in your organisation? How are these assessed and managed?*

IT GOVERNANCE AND ARCHITECTURE

In relation to business and IT alignment, it is important to consider both the IT governance and the enterprise architecture. These topics have become more prevalent in many organisations in recent years as the positive and negative impacts of IT have grown. This is because the role of IT has become embedded in the fabric of the organisation and the strategic nature of IT has been more evident.

IT governance

In understanding IT governance, a good starting point is to review corporate governance since this sets the overall governance framework and is potentially a key driver and provider of organisation principles. Corporate governance may be viewed as the alignment of the views and beliefs of organisation stakeholders to ensure accountability for meeting both strategic goals and operational duties.

In comparison, the IT Governance Institute[8] defines IT governance as:

> 'A structure of relationships and processes to control the enterprise in order to achieve the enterprise's goals by adding value while balancing risk versus return over IT and its processes.'

There are two key objectives implied by this definition which are consistent with the corporate governance perspective. The first goal is to ensure that the investments in IT generate business value. The second goal is to balance the risks associated with IT.

These goals can be supported by implementing an organisational structure with clear responsibility and processes for programmes and services involving information, business processes, applications and technology components.

Many organisations set up steering and prioritisation groups for programmes and projects. They recognise that there are competing demands for the same limited resources, often relating to IT staff and budgets. These groups share knowledge in order to assess which business projects are likely to add the most business value given the defined capacity and to determine which changes need to be implemented for legislative or risk reasons.

There may also be groups responsible for the individual components. Some organisations have set up a Technical Design Authority to monitor the introduction and management of new technologies into the organisation. Without this type of governance, individual business units or functions may purchase their own equipment without any regard to how this fits with the corporate infrastructure and purchasing agreements.

Other organisations have established similar groups for information and applications to ensure that the right choices are made at both the component and the integration level. This implies a longer-term vision for these components which is generated as part of the development of the enterprise architecture.

Enterprise architecture

The business change cycle recognises the importance of the alignment of business and IT strategy in the initial phase. An enterprise architecture is one of the tools to support alignment and build tomorrow's capability. It offers a conceptual blueprint that defines the structure and operation of an organisation. Potential advantages of the enterprise architecture include improved decision making, enhanced adaptability to changing demands or market conditions, elimination of inefficient and redundant processes, optimisation of the use of organisational assets and minimisation of employee turnover.

An enterprise architecture (EA) is a target model of the organisation covering both business components (processes and information) and technology components (applications and infrastructure). This definition leads us to the four main components of an EA:

(i) Business process architecture: outlines the organisation's key business processes and how they are linked.

(ii) Information architecture: defines the key elements of information subjects such as customers and transaction data such as orders plus the relationship between these elements.

(iii) Application architecture: defines and maps the relationships between software applications.

(iv) Technology infrastructure architecture: describes the components and grouping of hardware, operating systems and networks.

This four-component categorisation is broadly consistent with that of The Open Group Architecture Framework (TOGAF), which also has four components – business (or business process) architecture, data architecture, applications architecture, technology architecture. The Open Group website is a good source of material on architecture development[9].

There are other representations of an EA. One of the most well-known EA frameworks is the Zachman framework[10]. This model has two dimensions that relate the type of activity to key questions. There are six levels of type of architectural activity from contextual to operational (rows) and six core questions – what, how, where, who, when, why (columns).

Table 3.1 provides an interpreted extract of the Zachman framework rows covering the six architectural levels. These start with the scope which is of most interest to the planner and ends with the operational perspective of the user. Different model types support each layer. IT has historically focused on the system, technology and component levels of the Zachman framework whereas business change relates more to the scope and business model levels.

TABLE 3.1 *Extracted adaptation of Zachman framework*

	Architecture layer	Model type	Role
1	Scope	Contextual	Planner
2	Business model	Conceptual	Owner
3	System model	Logical	Designer
4	Technology model	Physical	Builder
5	Component model	Configurable	Implementer
6	Functioning enterprise	Operational	User

The first three of the six questions that cover the column headings most closely correspond to the four component EA view covering data, processes, applications and technology.

- **What** is primarily concerned with data.
- **How** is linked to both processes and applications.
- **Where** is linked to technology.

The Zachman framework combines these two dimensions of activity and questions, resulting in 36 cells of a matrix, which together represent the goals and structure of an organisation.

In recent years, architecture roles have become more prevalent and valued in organisations.

HEAD OF GOVERNANCE AND ARCHITECTURE

Robert Carr is the head of governance and architecture at Yell. He is responsible for a number of diverse yet related functions including enterprise architecture, programme office, quality, finance and security. His role is to ensure that both strategic and control perspectives are taken into account in the planning and delivery of IT-enabled business change and services.

Carr's view is that 'the architecture helps us build a strategic roadmap for the business and the governance ensures we follow the right route.'

IT-ENABLED CHANGE RISKS

In any major change, there are many significant risks that need to be evaluated and managed. As discussed, it is a necessary part of corporate and IT governance that there is an appropriate framework of accountabilities and processes in place to evaluate and address these risks.

You will find with most risk evaluation approaches, regardless of whether these relate to IT-enabled change, that there are structured steps involved in managing the risks. These include:

- identification of the risks and the possible impacts;
- assessment of the risks identified in terms of their probability and severity of impact;
- decisions on those risks that are to be accepted because they are unlikely to occur or will have minimum impact or are too expensive to address;
- formulation of measures to avoid the risks or mitigate them if they should occur.

The first two steps relate to the identification and evaluation of risk and the next steps represent responses and actions for dealing with risk.

Evaluating risk

One tool for evaluating risk is the 'heat map' shown in Figure 3.5.

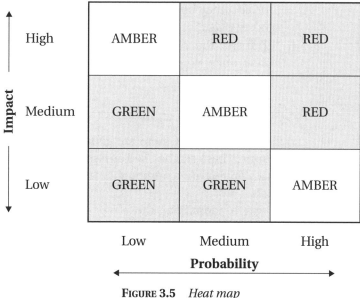

FIGURE **3.5** *Heat map*

Each risk is assessed as high, medium or low on the two dimensions of the probability of the risk materialising and the severity of the impact if it does. If either or both of these are high then the risk needs to be the subject of high attention. This is represented in the heat map by the red cells.

A different response is usually appropriate if either the probability or the severity is low and the other is not high in which case there is typically less of a concern, represented by the green cells in the heat map. Risk managers may allocate numbers to the probability and severity and then multiply these to give a risk assessment that can be calculated and stored in a spreadsheet.

Decisions on risk

The following are potential responses to the risk based on the results of the evaluation.

(i) Accept the risk. If the risk is in the green part of the heat map and any action to address the risk is costly it may be best to accept the consequences of an issue arising. Organisations may sometimes accept the risk when they assess the probability as fairly low but the impact is very high. This can be costly as some organisations have suffered major losses when the IT-enabled business change has failed.

(ii) Avoid the risk. Sometimes action can be taken which will reduce the probability of the risk occurring. If a new technology is being made available an organisation may not want to be the first to implement it.

(iii) Mitigate the impact. Where it is not possible to avoid the risk it may be possible to lessen the impact. The loss of a key person on the project may be alleviated if some degree of knowledge sharing has taken place.

(iv) Transfer the risk. It may be possible, for example, to take out insurance which effectively transfers the risk for an agreed premium.

Types of IT-enabled change risk

Experience shows that there are generic risks in any IT-enabled change programme. These can be used as a starting point to establish the specific risks in an organisation, although it is important not to adopt a formulaic approach.

One way of identifying these types of risks is through a classification approach. For example, the risks will vary depending on the stage of the IT-enabled business change life cycle. There will also be risks that can be categorised, for example, under the groupings of people, organisation and technology. There are some generic people-based risks, which relate to business engagement, user training and IT skills. These can have a further impact on the organisation and technology risks as described in the following examples.

(i)   Obtaining insufficient input from business users in the business improvement phase may result in requirements not being properly captured and this may be realised only during user acceptance testing in the implementation stage.

(ii) If people are not properly trained in the implementation phase this may result in a less effective business process and more difficulty in gaining the anticipated payback in the benefits phase.

(iii) A lack of knowledge of a purchased application package in the design phase may lead to set-up problems that become evident during testing in the implementation phase.

There are many examples in the media and published reports of IT-enabled change not delivering the expected benefits and in the short-term at least ending up with a situation that is worse than the starting point. As an example, see the brief case story below which relates to a UK home furniture retailer, MFI, who embarked on a major change programme with a heavy reliance on a new IT system.

IT-ENABLED BUSINESS CHANGE RISKS

MFI expects to save up to £35m a year once the five-year IT overhaul, which centres around a company-wide SAP roll-out, is completed in 2005. MFI has already invested £14m in the IT revamp project; it will invest a further £5m to £10m to 2005.

Source: *Computer Weekly*, 23 September 2003

There was a further update on this IT-enabled business change project a year later.

MFI has begun urgent remedial work on its £50m SAP-based supply chain system after warning that unexpected problems with the newly installed software would materially affect its profits. The home furnishings retailer warned that its UK retail division would show a substantial loss following the discovery of 'significant issues' with the system, affecting its ability to dispatch customer orders. A further £30m is needed to correct mistakes in orders delivered to customers and to put the SAP-based project back on track.

A SAP spokesman said, 'There is no problem with our software. It is not a software issue.'

Source: *Computer Weekly*, 13 September 2004

This is an example demonstrating that serious IT-enabled business change problems can also occur with private sector organisations.

POINT TO PONDER

Do you agree with the SAP representative that the problem in MFI was not a software issue?

One of the questions raised by the MFI example is whether this situation could have been avoided with the appropriate IT governance. It was reported that both the finance director and the operations director lost their jobs as a result of the problems with the implementation. This demonstrates very clearly the importance of senior management engagement and commitment to IT-enabled business change.

IMPORTANCE OF SENIOR MANAGEMENT COMMITMENT

We have seen that business and IT alignment involves many key choices. There are some issues that should not just be left to the IT department to resolve and the growth in importance of IT governance demonstrates that this is being taken on board. The senior management of an organisation need to evaluate how critical IT is to their strategic goals and operational survival. However, there is more to senior management commitment than just good stewardship. An active role is required in key business and IT decisions that may affect the future of the organisation.

How does a senior manager know which decisions are critical? It is not easy but if there is a commitment to developing a business vision of how the organisation should operate it is easier to map the IT decisions onto this target vision. Sometimes IT staff will complain about a lack of vision from senior managers who may be perceived to focus on short-term results rather than a long-term strategy. While this may be an accurate representation, it is the responsibility of IT management to engage with their business colleagues to understand both the immediate business goals and to help them define an aligned strategy for the future. The timing is important here in that sometimes an organisation has to focus on the short term, for example because of cost pressures or a recent acquisition, while at other times there is more time and need to focus on looking ahead. The important point is to gain senior management commitment for the actions required to both achieve the short-term goals and to develop the longer-term strategy.

COMMITMENT AND TIMING IN PRACTICE

While operating as a business systems director for a leading multinational I was asked to take on the role of IT director for the Italian subsidiary and to lead a major change programme following the acquisition of another large Italian company. What surprised our Italian team was that at the same time as creating a merged organisation Head Office also split the company into four divisions, each with a new managing director. This was because this structure matched its defined target business model.

It was evident that this major restructuring necessitated a rethink of the business strategy, structure and processes. However, in the short term we had tough financial targets arising from the acquisition plus an IT platform that was inflexible and costly. My focus and that of the other executives needed to be on delivery of the business change and results. Due to the complex nature of the reorganisation this required a strong commitment and focus from both the Italian divisions and the European Head Office.

After the implementation there was the time and the opportunity to conduct the strategic review, engaging the whole of the senior management team in Italy. I agreed the process with the Italian and European managing directors, bringing in a respected adviser from a

(Continued)

(Continued)

prestigious Italian business school as a facilitator. The approach to the planning and workshop was novel for this subsidiary and very well received. Paradoxically my assignment in Italy ended with a new business strategy, having started with the implementation of a challenging programme. While not a classic approach it did demonstrate that in order to engage top management in strategy development, timing is everything.

In the above example IT was fundamental to the success of the change programme and this was accepted by both Italian and European management. It is, however, important not to overplay the role of IT in areas which are not critical to the business operations. Organisations that consider that they neither have nor need a core competence in IT sometimes decide it is better to outsource the IT operations, and possibly development, to a third-party specialist. This can of course apply to any non-core business capability.

OUTSOURCING

This final part of the chapter considers one of the most important alignment issues for an organisation from both a business and an IT perspective. Outsourcing occurs where certain capabilities needed by the organisation to meet its business goals are subcontracted to other organisations. These may be business or IT capabilities. One of the initial drivers was to outsource functions that were seen as non-critical and that could be performed more cheaply or better by a specialist provider. The payroll of an organisation is a prime example of a business function that many organisations subcontract to a third party. Key reasons are that the third party specialises in the tax changes and there is no competitive impact from outsourcing the payroll, assuming that the correct amounts are paid to employees.

Outsourcing the payroll is an example of business process outsourcing (BPO). Another type is IT outsourcing, which has been evaluated or implemented or both by many organisations in recent years. IT outsourcing can be defined as the contracting to a third-party supplier of one or more IT functions such as data centre management, networking, hardware maintenance, software support, help desk and applications development.

There are many reasons that organisations outsource, which have emerged from a range of surveys. Results from one survey[11] showed the top five reasons as being:

(i)   reduce and control operating costs;
(ii) improve company focus;
(iii) free resources for other projects;

(iv) gain access to world class capabilities;

(v) resources not available internally.

Cost reduction is usually a key driver for outsourcing and it is no surprise to see this as the top driver although increasingly organisations appreciate the importance of other factors.

One of the least popular reasons for outsourcing was having a function that was difficult to manage or control. This is encouraging since this is generally not a solid base for moving services to a third-party supplier. The challenges when an organisation chooses this option include the difficulty of managing the outsourced supplier when there has been a failure to manage IT in-house and the complexity of establishing true comparative costs.

The internal IT group can develop systems that are used to track the performance of an outsourced operation. One particular goal is to monitor the agreed service levels of an outsourced logistics operation. Further, the internal IT group can provide the data communications which link the order processing group to the distribution centre. These two illustrations exemplify the prior discussion on the impact of IT, covering both business information and business operations.

Governance and risks of outsourcing

If a department is not perceived as being efficient or effective it is tempting for the chief executive to outsource the operation to a third party, but, as highlighted, there will be issues if the internal management is weak. One major risk that often materialises is that costs rise significantly due to requirements changes that are almost inevitable in a large programme. It is advisable to clarify and build into the contract pricing the potential areas of change. These may originate from different sources, such as internal business reasons or regulatory changes.

The governance in relation to outsourcing should deal with responsiveness to change and operational matters such as performance failure escalation. Service level agreements can only be explicit on accountability for those matters where the boundary is clear (and they should certainly be defined in these instances). However, performance issues such as response times may be due to decisions taken by both the organisation and the outsourcer.

It is important in these cases that the two organisations work in partnership in defining the key performance indicators and what will happen if the results fall outside the acceptable limits; in particular, who will be involved from the two parties. Some outsourcing agreements are labelled as 'co-sourcing', which explicitly recognises that the overall arrangement and the results need to be shared.

There are some general points that affect all IT outsourcing arrangements. Others will vary depending on the organisation. For example, the importance of availability, security and quality of data will be more critical for operational and financial applications that are customer-facing. These are areas where penalties in the contract may need to be considered.

Moving from an in-house IT operation to an outsourced one can be costly and time-consuming, particularly if this involves staff transfers and migration of technology platforms. This needs careful planning and the costs need to be accounted for. It may seem unduly pessimistic but one of the areas that should be scoped at this stage is the effort, time and cost that would be needed to bring the operation back in-house or to transfer to another supplier. This might affect how the contract and the transition are implemented.

The step beyond outsourcing within the same country is to transfer the work to another country and this is known as off-shoring. India has been the most popular choice owing to a combination of cost and quality combined with ease of communication given that English is its primary language of education. However, this apparent equivalence of language has sometimes led to problems. It was George Bernard Shaw who said, 'England and America are two countries separated by the same language.' A common language does not mean a common culture and that applies across and between countries. One response to this position is to analyse the cultural differences, perhaps using a model such as Hofstede as a starting point. The need to understand culture is illustrated by the following example, which is a modified version and interpretation of an actual case.

OFF-SHORING CULTURAL CHALLENGES

A medium-sized German supplier had been working closely with a large German organisation for many years and was providing reliable outsourced IT applications for an important part of the business. It was also able to deliver changes to these applications and to help integrate the changes into the infrastructure.

When the German organisation acquired a Canadian company it was decided that the German supplier would provide similar services although with a new version of the application developed by an Indian IT supplier. This turned out to be very problematic in that the Canadian company had an entrepreneurial style that was a challenge for the German supplier used to working in a process-driven culture. The Indian supplier was even more process-mature but the mixture of 'doing things by the book' and a 'good news' culture meant that requirements had to be very explicit and problems were only discovered when commitments could no longer be met.

It took some time to resolve these problems and it was only the choice to invest in strong on-site relationship building with both the Canadian company and the Indian supplier that led to the eventual success of the new operation.

The fact that there is now much more experience of outsourcing and off-shoring means that organisations are less likely to make strategically risky decisions without a thorough analysis. It is vital for the long-term health of an organisation that the decisions are not taken purely based on IT or commercial factors alone. This means that the senior management of the organisation need to be fully involved in any outsourcing decision and committed to dealing with the consequences of that decision.

CASE STUDY QUESTIONS

Review the case study on Foods. First you should gain an overview of the case and then focus in particular on the drivers for change in the alignment stage. What are the characteristics of this case that make it an IT-enabled business change programme? Consider what were the main drivers of the change programme. Would the case for change have been as strong if there were only business or only IT drivers? What were the key roles that were set up for this programme? How well aligned are the goals in the first stage? What risks need to be managed?

SUMMARY

This chapter has covered the first stage of the IT-enabled business change life cycle, business and IT alignment. This stage is often the least well managed since it requires a strategic and evolving understanding of the organisation's goals in relation to the external environment. It involves the engagement of multiple stakeholders, who often have different and conflicting viewpoints.

The nature of this challenge is different from the later more structured approaches associated with the development of the business solution. Making the wrong decision at this stage will have a knock-on effect at later stages and may require revisiting this stage. This will also be required if there are major external or internal 'shocks' that necessitate a shift in direction during the course of the change programme.

We have broadly covered the following topics.

TOPICS: BUSINESS AND IT ALIGNMENT

This chapter begins to study the hard (technological) and soft (people and culture) issues that impact on an organisation's effectiveness and which have to be carefully addressed to ensure success of an IT project. It provides the reader with an understanding of the interactions between IT and organisational performance. It covers:

- External and internal business environments for organisations:
  - ✦ the importance of understanding external environment influences;
  - ✦ the importance of analysing the internal organisational capability;
  - ✦ the importance of understanding culture.
- The positive and negative impacts of IT on organisations:
  - ✦ the use of IT to improve business operations;
  - ✦ the use of IT to improve business information.
- Effective linkage of IT governance and architecture.
- The risks of introducing IT-enabled business change.
- The importance of senior management commitment.
- The outsourcing business model.

SAMPLE QUESTIONS

Question 8

Which of the following are represented by the two Es of PESTLE?

- (i) External factors.
- (ii) Environment factors.
- (iii) Economic factors.
- (iv) External events.

- (a) ii, iii.
- (b) i, iii.
- (c) i, iv.
- (d) ii, iv.

Discussion

All of the factors in PEST and PESTLE are external factors but the E represents the individual factors. The economic factors are represented by the E of PEST, the original formulation. Environment was added later with legal to form PESTLE.

Question 9

Businesses are motivated by different targets at different levels within the organisation. Which of the following best represents a top-down sequential description of these motivations?

- (a) Mission, objective, strategy.
- (b) Strategy, mission, objective.
- (c) Mission, strategy, objective.
- (d) Objective, mission, strategy.

Discussion

This is a straightforward question if you are familiar with the acronym MOST to reflect the hierarchy of goals within an organisation.

Question 10

What is **not** an example of a risk arising from an IT-enabled business change?

- (a) Poor response time resulting from moving to online order entry.
- (b) Limited training and use of new compliance system.
- (c) Disaster recovery plan fails due to changes in phone numbers.
- (d) Poor information flows hinder redesigned processes.

Discussion

A disaster recovery plan should exist in any organisation independently of business changes. The question implies that this is the case and that the change is an administrative (although important) one in the contact numbers.

Question 11

Which of the following reasons best explains why it is strategically important to evaluate organisational capability?

 (a) To identify where there are job roles that need to be filled.
 (b) To scope the ability to respond to external opportunities.
 (c) To allocate responsibility for business change programmes.
 (d) To define the hardware resources for an IT-enabled project.

Discussion

Capability needs to be evaluated at different points in the IT-enabled business change life cycle. From a strategic perspective it is important to assess the ability to respond to external opportunities before scoping the change programme.

4 Business Improvement

The whole is more than the sum of its parts.

Aristotle in the *Metaphysics*

INTRODUCTION TO BUSINESS IMPROVEMENT DEFINITION

Let us assume that success has been achieved in the alignment stage. Hence there will be a broad stakeholder consensus on the size of the strategic opportunity and an initial scope of what is required to deliver the benefits. Now, at the business improvement stage, the organisation needs to define the gap between current state and target outcomes in more concrete terms. This will lead to a business case which quantifies the costs and benefits and evaluates the options for delivering the desired outcomes with the associated risks. The business case should also define the areas of required change and how to manage these as a programme. The structure of these component parts is shown in Figure 4.1.

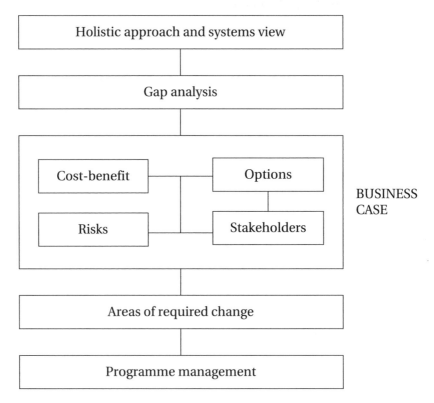

FIGURE 4.1 *Structure*

The tendency in many organisations is to move too quickly to a technical view of the solution where the output is defined in IT terms and all the other areas such as people, processes and information are constrained by the IT solution. What is needed is a more holistic approach – an understanding of the whole – in relation to business improvement. There is a connection between a holistic approach to business improvement and systems thinking. One of the leading people in this field, Peter Checkland, has commented that systems thinking can be viewed as the paradigm of thinking in a holistic way. Systems thinking is a contrast to the scientific method, which focuses on reducing the object of investigation into parts, i.e. reductionism. This chapter introduces the distinction between hard and soft systems; the latter focuses on people aspects and less structured systems.

SYSTEMS THINKING AND THE HOLISTIC APPROACH

Taking a systemic view

Utilising a systems thinking approach helps to give a broad perspective of the business objectives and the delivery of the IT-enabled business change. It is not about designing an IT system at this stage since the focus remains on analysing the business change.

Systems thinking enables us to describe and analyse the drivers and interrelationships that shape the behaviour of systems. Taking a holistic perspective allows us to analyse the complexity of relationships between the components, as compared with the reductionism approach, where the aim is to analyse the detailed components.

Systems thinking applied to IT-enabled business change means that we need to understand how the component parts fit together. In particular, we need to consider how processes, information, technology and people all interrelate to provide a workable business solution. It may be the case that an organisation has decided to introduce a computer system primarily for IT standardisation rather than for a direct

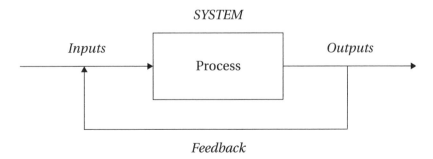

FIGURE 4.2 *System model*

business improvement, perhaps because the system is used by an acquiring organisation. However, even in this case, issues will arise if the new computer system is introduced into the organisation without a redesign of the way that the process works or if the staff are not trained on how to use it.

Systems regulate their state using feedback information about the output from the system, as shown in Figure 4.2.

There are different aspects to the way that feedback is generated in a business system. An organisation may have a business rule supporting feedback so that, for example, an invoice for a customer may lead to the credit limit being exceeded, which requires further action to be taken. Some computer systems are poorly documented and the business rules that form part of the feedback process are not clear.

Systems thinking can support a holistic understanding of the major gaps between the target and the current state of the business operation. At the business improvement stage the requirements will probably still be at a fairly high level although, ideally, sufficiently detailed to allow the key organisation and market decisions to be made that will impact on the business changes.

The systems thinking approach was originally applied to structured, quantifiable and technical 'hard' systems, although it has increasingly been applied to analysing more people-orientated and social 'soft' systems. Peter Checkland was the main driver behind the development of a soft systems methodology[12].

Soft systems methodology

Soft systems methodology (SSM) is particularly useful in the early stages of analysing the goals and requirements of a system. Its focus tends to be more on the people (soft factors) than the technology (hard factors). The methodology enables the application of systems thinking to develop a model of the real world. Many IS methods assume that systems can be engineered from start to finish. They take the objective of a system as a given input and establish how it is to be achieved. This 'hard' approach may fail when applied to less well-defined, or 'soft' situations, where establishing what is to be achieved is itself a major part of the problem.

The SSM approach considers different perspectives and uses these to derive a consensus model. This includes the use of a technique called CATWOE:

- Customer – everyone who stands to gain benefits from a system is considered as its customer, as are those who have a negative outcome. For example, if the system involves job losses then those affected must also be counted as customers.

- Actor – the actors perform the activities defined in the system in order to achieve the desired transformation.
- Transformation process – represents conversion from input to output in the system.
- Weltanschauung – the German expression for world view. This world view provides a context for the transformation process and defines the underlying belief from a particular perspective.
- Owner – the principle is that every system has an owner who has the power to start up and shut down the system and to make key decisions on the transformation.
- Environmental constraints – external elements exist outside the scope of the system and may result in constraints on the system. These constraints may include organisational policies as well as legal and ethical matters.

In describing these elements, the aim is to capture the richness of the reality through sketches or 'rich pictures' that describe rather than try to simplify a complex situation. SSM is divided into seven distinct stages to analyse the problem situation and generate recommended actions. A simplified view of the approach follows.

(i) Find out about the problem situation by asking questions such as, who are the key actors and what are the issues with how the process works today?

(ii) Express the problem situation through 'rich pictures' formed from the elements of CATWOE. This helps knowledge to be communicated visually.

(iii) Select how to view the problem situation using root definitions. The root definition is a way of describing the objective of a system from the viewpoint of a particular actor. As an example, a supermarket car park system may exist to organise spaces for the public by means of free tickets so as to encourage them to shop in the store.

(iv) Build conceptual models of what the system needs to do for each root definition.

(v) Compare the conceptual models with the real world. This involves reviewing the results from steps iv and ii to see where they differ and where they are similar.

(vi) Identify feasible and desirable changes to improve the situation.

(vii) Provide recommendations for taking action to improve the problem situation, including how to implement the changes identified in the previous step.

The rich pictures inherent in the soft systems methodology support a holistic view of the business problem and improvement.

Holistic approach to business improvement

One challenge in the business improvement definition stage is to add more detail without losing sight of the big picture. There are a number of deliverables required before moving to the design stage of the business change. The first of these is to describe the change in a way that makes sense to all the stakeholders, including the senior managers engaged in the alignment stage and the professionals responsible for the design stage.

Too often, we see IT-enabled business change projects labelled as the implementation of a particular technology. One particular example of this relates to enterprise resource planning (ERP) software, which is supplied by organisations such as SAP and Oracle. ERP has been around for many years and has a particular attraction for business managers in that it offers an integrated view across many operational functions such as sales, manufacturing and finance. Where the problem arises is if the focus of the change switches from the overall business improvement to the implementation of the software. A warning signal occurs when the change is labelled as the technology, for example 'the SAP project'. The strong recommendation is to maintain a focus on the organisation, process and people aspects of the business improvement.

EXAMPLE OF A HOLISTIC APPROACH

A consumer products organisation has recognised through research that more of its customers have access to the internet. In particular, the business and IT alignment analysis has identified that this organisation wishes to allow its customers to order its products online as an add-on facility to ordering via a sales person or telesales call centre.

Given that an internet facility is not currently provided, this will require substantial business and IT changes with potential implications for people and systems performing the existing operations. Key decisions will need to be taken that will depend on the business strategy. Will all the products be provided online? Will the same customers be targeted? What pricing strategy will be adopted? Will this be set up as a separate operation? Is it expected that this will lead to a growth in sales or will there be a reduction in existing sales staff? How will queries be handled?

These decisions and others will have an impact on the options for handling the business change. Should the internet service be provided in-house or via a third party? Will the existing customer and product data files be used or will new ones be set up? Which people will be trained up to answer the queries from customers? How will any staff reductions be handled?

It can be seen from the example that many decisions have to be taken on how to implement the business improvement. A decision process is needed to evaluate those options which will have a significant impact on the design of the business change. Typically this will involve considering costs, benefits, time and risks plus other criteria such as the quality of the potential supplier. The costs and benefits of the selected option will then form part of the business case for the proposed solution.

The likely size and complexity of the change should have been identified at the alignment stage. If the change is a substantial one, a programme management approach should be evaluated for the improvement stage. Within the overall programme there will be projects or streams of activity. This again supports a holistic approach to the business improvement while managing the diverse elements such as business and technical components.

GAP ANALYSIS

Gap analysis is the process of assessing the gap that has to be bridged between where an organisation is now and where it wants to be. While (nearly) all organisations are striving to improve their performance, the degree of ambition and capability varies between organisations. There are also different drivers for change that influence the size of the gap between the goal and the current state. One tool that can provide a guide to the level of change required is the model of IT-enabled business transformation, which has five levels categorised by Venkatraman (1994). The levels provide a guide on the effort required to move from a current to a desired state. The five levels in the model include two evolutionary and three revolutionary levels:

	Level
Evolutionary	
Localised exploitation	1
Internal integration	2
Revolutionary	
Business process redesign	3
Business network redesign	4
Business scope redefinition	5

These levels represent increasing levels of business change and benefits. The first level of a **local exploitation** may involve the introduction of a specific system such as a sales support package within a customer services environment. Moving from local exploitation to **integration** may include a replacement of existing legacy systems by an integrated package such as an ERP system. Integrated applications can provide the enabler for the third level of **business process redesign** (BPR), which relates to the internal design of an organisation. The fourth level, **business network redesign**, is associated with changing the relationship with external customers and suppliers. The fifth and highest level in the business transformation model is the use of IT to **redefine the business scope**. An example of this is where IT becomes integral to the product in such a way that it changes the whole nature of the business.

An organisation that is aiming to move up more than one level will have a bigger gap to close than one that is moving up one level. On the other hand, it is useful to have a target to aim for as this may influence the journey. For example, many organisations have found it difficult to implement an ERP system at the same time as re-engineering their business processes. However, some organisations who have implemented an ERP have found that they have embedded the old processes and found it difficult to change these processes later. One way to address this issue is to start with a redesign of the business processes as a guide to the ERP implementation and select which process changes need to be made first.

In the alignment stage strategic gaps will have been evaluated to define the broad scope of the initiative. In the business improvement stage more detail is required on where the gaps are and how the gaps can be closed as an input to scoping the solution options and the business case.

Various requirements-elicitation techniques are available to understand and map the current and desired state in order to understand the requirements and define the gaps:

- Document analysis – reviewing relevant documents for background on the current situation and to gain information on strategic goals and constraints.
- Interviews – usually semi-structured discussions that help the analyst to understand individual needs and personal perspectives.
- Workshops – interactive forums in which ideas can be discussed and consensus reached on where the organisation is now and where it needs to be.
- Observation – viewing how people perform business processes and assessing their issues in doing so.

These information-gathering approaches may be supported by selected business modelling techniques that aim to capture the 'as is' (current) and 'to be' (future target) views of the organisation using a structured approach. Creating business models enables stakeholders to review and discuss critical organisation ways of working and the required improvements. There are many different business modelling techniques and examples of these such as process and information models will be covered in more detail in the next chapter.

In the business improvement stage of the IT-enabled business change the intention is not to detail all the requirement gaps. The challenge is to capture the key ones which will impact and feed into the design stage. For example, take a current process which is based on customers phoning a call centre for information and a desired state which allows customers to obtain answers to their queries via a website. It will be important to understand what user interface will be required and what types of query the user will be able to answer online. It will not be necessary to define in detail the text that comprises all of the answers since this can be done at a later stage without a major impact on costs, benefits, time and risks.

The level of detail from the gap analysis should be sufficient to determine the scope of the changes impacting the organisation, people, processes, information and technology, which are the components covered in the next chapter on business change design.

Once the current position, target position and gap have been identified different options can be identified to close the gap. There will often be significant differences in the degree of change required for these options and this will be considered in the following section on the business case.

BUSINESS CASE

Contents of a business case

The business case consolidates much of the information gathered to-date on the problem or gap, options, solution and cost-benefit. Contents of an IT-enabled change business case are likely to include some or all of the following elements.

(i) Drivers for change:
- organisational background including strategic perspective;
- problems and opportunities with the current processes and systems.

(ii) Proposed business solution:
- evaluation of options and recommended solution;
- components of the solution.

(iii) Implementation approach:
- project management approach, governance and timescales;
- success criteria and risk management.

(vi) Cost-benefit analysis:
- total cost of ownership – business and IT;
- return on investment and strategic justification.

Some might argue that an implementation approach is not needed in a business case; however, if this is not done, it will be difficult to accurately determine the costs and the risks. Furthermore, the fact that this has been considered is likely to increase the credibility of the case and the person proposing the case. It is a good discipline to prepare a one-page executive summary of these key points and some organisations insist on this being done.

Identifying and evaluating options

The options to meet the goals of the business change programme need to be identified and evaluated according to agreed criteria. There should always be a 'do nothing or do little' option which represents remaining with the current state and provides a base case for the cost-benefit analysis. Figure 4.3 shows the role of options and linkage to the business case.

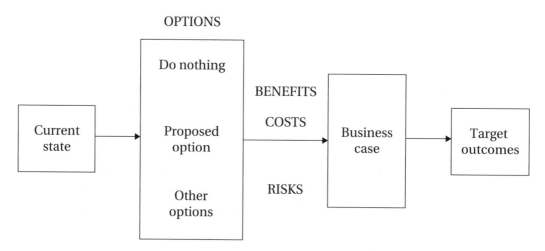

OPTIONS

Do nothing

BENEFITS

COSTS

Current state → Proposed option → Business case → Target outcomes

Other options

RISKS

FIGURE 4.3   *Options*

The number of options to be presented and the criteria for evaluating these options will vary depending on the situation. Often there will be a range of incremental options between 'do nothing' and 'do everything' to achieve the outcomes with different levels of costs and benefits. For example, creating a business intelligence solution may focus on the critical analyses required by the organisation or attempt to build an all-encompassing solution.

This 'do everything' solution may be delivered in one implementation as a 'big bang' option. There is also the possibility of scoping the total solution but reaching it through incremental phases potentially with each phase having its own business case. This evolutionary option will take longer to deliver the benefits but it also means that the costs will be staggered.

Identifying, evaluating and presenting options are key challenges in an IT-enabled change programme. Deciding between options can be a difficult task and one where there is often disagreement between the stakeholders. How can you move the discussion from a subjective and personal viewpoint to one that is seen as objectively in the organisation's best interests? The recommended tactic is to agree the criteria for making the choice at an early stage in the decision-making process, which adds a degree of transparency to the selection process. If appropriate, different weights can be assigned to these criteria.

As described above, two of the key criteria are the level of costs and benefits of the different options. Other potential criteria to be assessed relate to the longer-term sustainability of the solution. In the case of a purchased solution or component, this includes the quality of the supplier and the product. These are not necessarily the same. The organisation may conclude that the product is not the best in the marketplace but if the evaluation team is more confident that the supplier will still be around in future years that may be enough to sway the decision to this longer-term supplier.

Analysing risks and trade-offs associated with options

One of the key factors to consider is the comparative risk associated with each of the options. There will be risks associated with the level and timing of costs and benefits. Additionally, a 'do everything' and 'big bang' type of solution will have a high risk associated with it since the outcome may be one **that** has a very negative impact on the performance of the organisation. The example of MFI covered in a previous chapter demonstrates what can happen when a major implementation has problems. However, the alternative to a 'big bang' solution can also be high risk.

EXAMPLE

One major change programme that I enabled from an IT leadership role involved the takeover of another organisation. This required restructuring the whole operation including the sales, order processing and logistics functions. Any failure would have a dramatic effect on revenue yet the alternative was to delay restructuring and have a de-motivated workforce, which would also impact revenue. Fortunately the 'big bang solution' worked in this case.

In the previous chapter, types of IT-enabled business change risks were considered, in particular people, organisation and technology. This classification may also be useful in comparing options in the business case. A related input to risk analysis is to consider the success criteria for the IT-enabled business change. These may for example include acceptance of the change by a user community. Therefore if one of the options has a potentially negative impact on this user community, the risk needs to be assessed and considered in the evaluation of options.

Any major change involves risks with the delivery. These project risks may be expressed as those associated with time (delays), budget (overruns) and specification (scope or quality). Often there is a potential trade-off between these three elements; for example, a delay may be avoided by spending more on external resources or by reducing the specification.

It is advisable to build in a contingency for one or more of these risks. In the case of the costs, there may be an explicit contingency budget. If a time contingency is appropriate, there may be a target date set but with the flexibility to implement on a later delivery date. If there is no possibility or desire to have contingencies on time and cost there may be an opportunity to reduce the scope of the specification by leaving out some non-critical feature. The choice of contingency will depend upon the particular context for the project.

POINT TO PONDER

The Olympics 2012 will be held in London, England. Most previous Olympics have gone over budget and a programme contingency budget for Olympics 2012 was set at over two billion pounds. Which contingency option clearly is not appropriate in this scenario?

Cost-benefit analysis

The majority of business cases need to have a return on investment (ROI) where the anticipated financial benefits exceed the estimated costs. It is important that the business case includes the costs and benefits of the full business solution, not just the IT components.

These costs include set-up and ongoing costs. The upfront costs are those that are normally incurred as a one-time investment since they relate to the set-up of components such as the new process, system, training and databases. For example, deciding to upgrade the system that performs the financial accounting of the organisation may involve the purchase of a new application package. Once these components are in place there will be a cost to upgrade and maintain them, such as the annual maintenance costs for an application package.

Some examples of items that generate IT costs are as follows:

(i) Hardware – the equipment on which the IT application software will run.

(ii) Software – the purchased software.

(iii) Development – the development of software.

(iv) Conversion – the time and costs involved in the systems conversion.

(v) Maintenance – the ongoing maintenance of the software.

(vi) Operations – the cost of running the system (may be higher or lower than existing).

Business costs will be generated by the following items:

(i) Requirements – this is the cost of gathering requirements, which involves the time of business managers and business actors as well as the business analyst.

(ii) Training – this includes the preparation time for creating training material and the time for both trainers and those being trained.

(iii) Process change – this is the time and effort involved in understanding and changing the business processes.

(iv) Data quality – the importance of accurate data and the challenges of converting it from one system to another are sometimes underestimated.

(v) User guides – preparation of documentation, both paper and online.

(vi) Support – help desk and on-site support for business users.

Sometimes organisations do not include the business costs in a business case because they view that the work is being performed by permanent employees and therefore no extra cost is seen to be incurred. However, there is always an opportunity cost for this work since other activities could be performed. Furthermore, when this resource is needed there may be conflicting demands. If a budget has been made available one option is to bring in temporary staff either to perform these activities or to carry out the operational duties, releasing staff to work on the change project.

The business case benefits may arise in a number of areas of the business including the IT function. Some of the key areas to look for benefits are:

(i) lower operating cost arising from improvements in efficiency;

(ii) reduced level and cost of holding inventory;

(iii) improved data accuracy leading to fewer errors and customer issues;

(iv) reduced risks, for example related to information security;

(v)   flexibility for growth supporting increased business volumes;

(vi) improved customer service levels;

(vii) increased sales volume and value;

(viii)faster time to market with a product or service ;

(ix) enhanced employee morale.

The aim is to put a financial number to each benefit although this is sometimes difficult to do. This issue will be addressed further in the chapter on benefits management.

Engaging stakeholders in the business case

The business case needs to be an objective document that presents well-argued reasons for investment supported by sound evidence. Most business case presentations need to provide a credible set of quantifiable costs and benefits even if these are not the only or even the main reason for the proposed investment. However, a viable set of numbers is rarely enough for a business case to be accepted at face value. Ultimately it is the senior stakeholders that accept the business case and they are looking for people they trust to accurately represent and deliver what is proposed in the business case.

How many options should be presented to the executive team responsible for making the final decision on the investment? There is no one right answer to this; however, it can be said that one option is effectively 'no option'. In this case the decision may be to 'do nothing'. That is why it is recommended that a do little scenario be evaluated and the implications presented as an option. In particular, the financial and non-financial consequences of this option should be well understood and articulated rather than an assumption made that everyone accepts that the situation is dire and that change needs to happen. The risk here is that there may be a strong supporter who does not have sufficient power in the organisation to gain acceptance for the business case, especially if there are others who oppose the change.

The stakeholder analysis described in the business and IT alignment chapter will have identified those who have the power and interest to review the business case as well as potential supporters and opposers of the change. This should specifically be reviewed to consider whether changes have taken place in the stakeholders and their positioning. It can then be used to target individuals who will have a say in the acceptance of the business case.

Where feasible it is useful to meet with the key stakeholders in advance of the business case being formally presented. Each stakeholder is likely to have a different view of the critical factors based on the role they perform. For example, a finance director will normally be supportive of a business case that has a short payback period or reduces working capital. In contrast, the customer services and sales directors will probably consider the effect on customer satisfaction and the consequent impact on sales if the proposed changes are implemented.

AREAS OF REQUIRED CHANGE

Moving to the next stage requires a definition of the gaps, options, proposed solution and implementation approach. These all help to define the required areas for change and the relative size of these areas within the overall programme. Yet there is a tendency for organisations to structure and resource the programme with the technology components of IT applications and infrastructure taking a more prominent role than the other components needed for success.

At one level, this is understandable since the IT investment is usually more visible with external expenditure on hardware, software and consultants. The danger is that the other changes in processes, people and data are relatively under-resourced particularly if there are later cost increases in the technology components. Few organisations seem to fully recognise the interdependencies in this relationship. If less investment is made in engaging people to redesign the processes and improve the data quality there is often a knock-on effect on the technology delivery, which has to go through more iterations than predicted.

Therefore getting the balance right between the areas of change is critical. This will not be the same for each programme. Moving from one technology platform to another will probably have an impact on data migration, training people and business continuity processes but these will be relatively smaller components. In a major organisation change there may be some changes in reporting data hierarchies and IT security access but the biggest changes will be in people and, potentially, processes.

Information and data management are key components of the change. Creating an organisation-wide business scorecard requires a major focus on understanding the information requirements then ensuring that the results are delivered to trained and motivated people through the appropriate processes. Depending on the existing systems platform the extract of data might be a relatively simple or a very time-consuming task.

The resourcing of the programme will be influenced by the size and complexity of each of the areas of change. This will determine the level of resource needed in the design and implementation stages. The selection of the programme manager may reflect the dominant expertise needed to effect the change. As with the choice of project managers, this can sometimes be a tough decision. If someone is strong in IT and average in project management, is this preferable to a strong project manager who has little knowledge of IT? It will be important to consider the overall mix of the team and then to put in place development and support plans for those people who need it.

Consultancy skills

A key skill required in the team is that of consultancy. The business improvement stage is one where consultancy skills are particularly important given the need to agree objectives with a variety of stakeholders. External consultants may be hired to give independent expert advice in IT or business change. Additionally, internal or external consultants may be tasked to help analyse and define the requirements of business users.

The ISEB Certificate in IS Consultancy Practice lists the following outcomes from its course:

- Understanding the role of the consultant in the IT/IS industry.
- Awareness of IT issues in the business context.
- Planning and managing their client relationships over the consultancy life cycle.
- Scoping, proposing and contracting of consultancy assignments.
- Structuring, planning and controlling consultancy assignments.
- Dealing with difficult client issues.
- Appreciating human personality and responding appropriately to behaviour issues.
- Problem solving, communications and interpersonal skills specific to IS consultants.
- The application of quality control and measurement within IS consultancy assignments.

The syllabus is available via the ISEB website and covers a range of topics including managing client relationships, problem definition, communications and quality[13].

IMPORTANCE OF PROGRAMME MANAGEMENT

In the *Introduction* chapter, one definition given for a change programme was to deliver an improved strategic capability through a set of interdependent projects. In the *Glossary*, a programme is more generally defined as 'a collection of projects that is directed toward a common goal'.

The key point about both these definitions is that they recognise the need for a holistic approach to achieve an improved capability or goal and also that this will be achieved through multiple projects. This is an important perspective which was highlighted in an earlier section of this chapter on the holistic approach to business improvement.

In a major IT-enabled business change there is a need to scope and plan multiple business and IT deliverables. This focus on interdependent change is what makes a programme management approach and capability necessary. One potential structure of a programme is where project managers are appointed for the business process, people, information and technology sets of deliverables. Alternatively, there may be several integrated business and IT deliverables, for example, combining a customer-facing project and an administrative project to provide a total business solution.

The programme manager is the person who is accountable for overseeing the suite of projects that will deliver the business changes. The key element of this role is to ensure that all of the projects are co-ordinated and any dependencies between the projects are identified and managed.

Programme management encompasses the activities of defining, planning, controlling and completing programmes. This set of activities is different from but complementary to that of IT-enabled business change. There is not a fixed point when a programme structure is set up. The aim is to scope and plan the programme as soon as it becomes apparent that the IT-enabled business change requires this level of management. Although the timing of setting up a programme can vary, once the alignment stage has been completed a delivery focus can start to be applied to the business improvement stage. It is the responsibility of the programme manager to ensure that the IT-enabled business change has a delivery emphasis and this will include defining a number of elements.

Programme objectives should describe the business outcomes required to deliver the business benefits. The structure of the programme should be created with individual projects and deliverables. Ownership of the deliverables should be clearly defined, including both business and IT as well as external and internal accountabilities. The consolidation of these deliverables should be clearly linked to the overall outcomes and hence the benefits.

The programme manager needs to work with the business sponsor to ensure that the programme is correctly set up with a capable sponsoring group that includes different representatives from those affected by the IT-enabled business change. There will be a need to engage the sponsoring group in the allocation of resources, both business and IT, to achieve these goals. An appropriate programme governance structure will be required at the start and this may change as the programme evolves.

It can be seen that programme management is a critical role in this stage of the IT-enabled business change life cycle.

CASE STUDY QUESTIONS

Review the case study on Foods. First you should gain an overview of the case (if not already done) and then focus in particular on the business improvement stage.

What was the identified gap that the programme is designed to close? How have the improvement initiatives been scoped? Who are the stakeholders who have to buy into the business case and what approach do you believe is required?

SUMMARY

The chapter has covered the second stage of the IT-enabled business change life cycle. This stage of defining the business improvement marks the transition from alignment to a more detailed understanding of the required improvement. It needs a holistic understanding of the scope and benefits of the proposed improvement supported by a business case covering the costs, benefits and risk analysis.

These, with other selected criteria, will help to decide the best option for the business solution and outline the areas of required change so that these can be designed appropriately as covered in the business change design chapter.

The importance of programme management has been highlighted and this theme is also further developed in the next chapter, moving to the definition of the programme.

We have broadly covered the following topics.

TOPICS: BUSINESS IMPROVEMENT DEFINITION

The objective of this chapter is to provide an understanding of the business analysis approach to identifying business improvements. It introduces tools and approaches used to establish, to evaluate, plan and manage an IT-enabled business change programme. The topics cover:

- The principles of taking a systemic view.
- The holistic approach to business improvement.
- The principles of the gap analysis approach.
- The contents of the business case including the cost-benefit analysis.
- The need to identify and evaluate options for business change.

- The importance of risk analysis in evaluating options in the business case.
- Presenting a business case that engages and convinces the stakeholders.
- The range of areas where changes may be required.
- The importance of programme management to IT-enabled business improvement.

SAMPLE QUESTIONS

Question 12

It is important to take a systemic view of business change because:

(a) IT professionals understand systems and are the main group interested in business change;

(b) there are often interdependencies and interactions between IT systems;

(c) organisations are complex and change to one area is likely to impact upon other areas;

(d) IT systems are usually the key element in driving business change.

Discussion

The focus of this question is on business change rather than the interaction between systems or IT professionals.

Question 13

What is the terminology used to describe the process views that need to be mapped in a process redesign?

(a) 'Current' and 'possible'.

(b) 'Today' and 'to be'.

(c) 'As is' and 'to be'.

(d) 'As is' and 'planned'.

Discussion

This question is related to common terminology used for process redesign as shown in the *Glossary*.

Question 14

Which of the following financial terms are most likely to be used to link organisation benefits back to a business case?

(i) Net present value (NPV).

(ii) Market value adjustment.

(iii) Return on investment (ROI).

(iv) Payback.

(v) Deficiency payment.

(a) i, iii, iv.

(b) ii, iv, v.

(c) i, ii, iv.

(d) i, ii, iii.

Discussion

NPV, ROI and payback are the terms typically used in organisations for benefits evaluation. Market value adjustment and deficiency payment are other terms used in specific sectors.

Question 15

Which of the following roles is responsible for investigating and documenting business requirements?

   (a) Programme manager.
   (b) Business analyst.
   (c) Systems designer.
   (d) Business sponsor.

Discussion

The investigation and documentation of business requirements is done by the business analyst. The designer will take the requirements and create a systems design. The programme manager needs to ensure that the requirements are delivered within an appropriate time for this to happen. The sponsor needs to understand how the requirements will translate into business benefits.

Question 16

Which of the following would be identified in a business case as an intangible cost?

   (a) Licences for a new software package.
   (b) Loss of goodwill.
   (c) Hire of a consultant for a study lasting 10 days.
   (d) Purchase of a new telephone system.

Discussion

All of the above options apart from the loss of goodwill are direct financial costs that can be estimated with a degree of certainty.

Question 17

The project sponsor must always be:

   (a) a senior user of the IT systems affected by the change project;
   (b) the owner of the business case and responsible for its achievement;
   (c) a director of the business functions affected by the change project;
   (d) the head of the IT function working on the change project.

Discussion

The choice of sponsor may vary depending on the business circumstances and the capability of the individuals. It is possible that the sponsor may be a business director, senior user or the head of the IT function. Whatever the primary role, the sponsor must own the business case and its achievement.

Question 18

Which of the following options should always be considered when developing a business case for a new IT system?

(a) Outsourcing the IT function.
(b) Developing an IT system in-house.
(c) Redesigning a business process.
(d) Continuing with the current system.

Discussion

In considering options for change it is important to always evaluate the 'do nothing' option of continuing with the current system.

Question 19

Taking a 'holistic' view of business improvement means:

(a) taking an objective view when examining the range of possibilities for business changes;
(b) considering the organisational, process and human dimensions of change;
(c) looking for all of the problems with the current business operations;
(d) focusing on the 'soft' aspects related to any proposed business operations.

Discussion

Business improvement covers more than just addressing the operational problems as it seeks strategic opportunities. This means taking a broader perspective than either an 'objective' view or the 'soft' aspects of change.

5 Business Change Design

Things alter for the worse spontaneously, if they be not altered for the better designedly.

Francis Bacon 1561–1626

INTEGRATED BUSINESS CHANGE DESIGN

In the previous chapter the focus was on scoping the business improvement in a holistic way. The organisation needs to embrace and manage the change, which requires it to have the right structure and people in place to improve the business processes supported by appropriate information and technology components. Hence, the next stage in the IT-enabled business change life cycle is to construct a design of these individual components. It is also important to take an integrated approach to the design.

Figure 5.1 illustrates the integrated design of the organisation, people, process, information and technology components delivered through a programme design approach. This target picture defines the structure of this chapter.

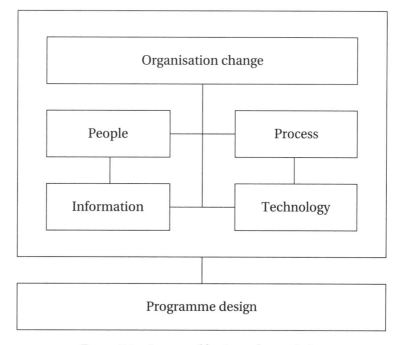

FIGURE 5.1 *Integrated business change design*

Sample deliverables from the business change design stage could include revised organisation performance measures, a set of revised business processes, a training programme, a new IT system and an updated information model.

These components together form a business solution which will need to be managed and co-ordinated in order to ensure the successful delivery of the programme. There is a distinction between the design of the business solution and the design of the programme to deliver it.

ASPECTS OF ORGANISATION CHANGE DESIGN

IT-enabled change requires both 'hard' and 'soft' elements of organisation design. The former includes the design of the organisation structure and a well-defined performance measurement system which is capable of analysing the work outcomes in quantified terms. The latter includes shaping an appropriate culture for the organisation and ensuring that the employees are skilled and motivated to perform the work. One element that links these two areas is designing the appropriate organisational incentives and key performance measures that will encourage the needed behaviours for effective change.

Organisation structure

A key decision for the organisation is to decide what work should be performed by the organisation and what work should be distributed to other sources outside of the organisational boundary. Introducing business change is an opportunity to reflect on what is the optimum mix of this work. Even if the work is to be directly carried out and managed by the organisation there is still the decision as to whether this will be done by full-time staff, part-time staff, contractors or consultants. Making this decision requires an analysis of the type of work and skills required over time. Organisations need to evaluate the management approach and overhead when comparing the costs and benefits of each option.

Performance measurement and management

Every organisation has some financial accounting responsibilities that reflect legislative demands. In the private sector, this will include reporting on the profitability of doing business and the investments in assets that help to maintain and enhance profits. In the public sector there will be accounting for asset investments and other costs. While these are important indicators of a healthy organisation they reflect what has happened in the past and do not cover every aspect of the business.

A key element of performance management relates to getting the best out of people, often referred to as an organisation's most important asset. The regular performance appraisal is a key part of the human resources procedure for many organisations. It should be viewed not only as a means to review past performance but also a valuable opportunity to align the individual, team and company objectives.

The design of an organisation's salary and compensation package is an important part of encouraging the right behaviours in a time of business change. Offering some form of recognition for engaging in and contributing to successful business improvements sends a clear message to all the employees. The incentives may be a mix of 'stick and carrot' with rewards and associated penalties. Sometimes a bonus based on performance can achieve both of these aims since the loss of a potential reward represents a penalty. However, there is a danger that a poorly defined incentive system may encourage behaviours that are not in the organisation's interest. A person who achieves a project deadline bonus or a call response time target is not necessarily helping the organisation if resulting quality problems lead to much higher costs.

Organisational culture

We have seen that the type of organisational culture can promote or hinder business change depending on what type of change is intended. There is likely to be a stronger buy-in when more detailed procedures are implemented in a bureaucratic culture than one that is highly entrepreneurial. Changing organisational culture is not straightforward. It is easier to destroy trust than to build it. Research suggests that there is a 'psychological contract' between an employer and employee which can become very strained if organisations are not seen to respect the needs and values of their employees.

ASPECTS OF PEOPLE DESIGN

Jobs and roles

A key link between organisation and people perspectives is the design of jobs and roles. Often a job may involve more than one role. For example, a business solutions manager who has responsibility for a defined area such as marketing has both business analysis and account management roles. It is important for the business solutions manager to understand the distinction and the overlap between these roles in order to perform both of these properly. If the marketing director has a short-term urgent problem such as not being able to correctly price a product due to a systems issue, the need is to respond quickly wearing the account management hat. Perhaps later it will be appropriate to point out where the pricing policy is not consistent and how this is leading to both IT and customer service issues.

Training and development needs

Often, in appointing staff to new roles and jobs, there will be recognition that the selected person has competence gaps that make it difficult to perform at the desired level. This generates a development need which should not be ignored. One response is to organise a short training course. Clearly this should be part of the overall development process rather than a stand-alone course that people join when there is money remaining in the training budget at the year-end. Opportunities should be created for the person attending the training to use and test the newly acquired skills. Ideally this will be done with a coach or mentor who has been through a similar process.

Additional support is particularly advisable if the training is for an interpersonal skill such as negotiation or influencing. If someone has a strong analytical bias they may find it hard to modify their behaviour and to focus as much on engaging the stakeholder as on the task in hand. A coach or mentor will be able to give prompt feedback on these interactions to reinforce good behaviours and reflect on what is going wrong in other situations.

Motivation and reward

A key part of the appointment to a new job is to consider the person's motivation to do well in the role. Skill alone is not enough. The careful design of an organisation's performance measurement and reward system can increase the motivation of the workforce, both managers and employees. However, it is important to recognise that each individual has their own personal motivations. Many factors such as working conditions, team spirit and the support of the first-level manager affect the commitment of a person to embrace significant change. A good leader will recognise these factors and will aim to flex the incentives within the organisation's human resources rules.

Engaging with human resources

The role of the human resources (HR) department varies between organisations. In some companies it is seen purely as an administration function dealing with legislative matters such as avoiding industrial tribunals. In other cases HR is at the forefront of organisation change providing leadership in creating a new culture and ways of working. Occasionally IT and HR report to the same executive director but this is the exception rather than the rule. Therefore a proactive stance is needed to engage the HR management in IT-enabled business change. It is advisable to give thought to specific people issues and requirements related to the programme in advance of this engagement. For example, the HR manager might be able to identify a potential programme or project manager by knowing what other organisation changes are planned in the next few months. If the IT and HR management are able to build this relationship it can lead to longer-term initiatives such as an organisation-sponsored course on project management or IT-enabled business change.

ASPECTS OF PROCESS CHANGE DESIGN

Differences between functions and processes

Organisations typically have a hierarchical structure based on business functions. Examples of these are: marketing, finance, operations, human resources and IT. One reason for this grouping is that it brings together people with similar skills who perform related activities with managerial guidance. It provides a clear promotion path for those in the function who can be evaluated by more senior people who have pursued a similar route. Often this progression is partly mapped out as part of a career development with membership of bodies such as the accounting and legal professions. The British Computer Society is making a significant effort to promote IT as a profession with a similar standing.

Typically the heads of each of the main functions sit on the top executive team of the organisation. Hence decisions made by this group incorporate and take advantage of a functional expertise as well as the general management capability that each functional head should possess. While this highlights why the functional structure is common, we also need to be aware of the disadvantages. In particular, the main business processes of an organisation are not carried out solely within functional silos.

The reality in organisations is that business processes require co-operation between functions and poor communications will lead to ineffective processes. Any issue with communications is accentuated in a multinational organisation or environment with partners from different countries and cultures. The spread of shared services, sometimes outsourced or offshore, provides scope for miscommunication if the processes are not clearly designed, including identification of what happens when events do not go according to plan.

CROSS-FUNCTIONAL PROCESS EXAMPLE

A typical business process in organisations is the purchasing of products and services through a specialist procurement department. If the marketing department has a requirement it needs to make a requisition, which, after approval, will go to the purchasing department to place the order with the supplier. Delivery is to the warehouse, which confirms receipt of goods. The purchase invoice is sent to an accounting

(Continued)

(Continued)

function to match the purchase order, goods received note and the invoice before making the payment.

Marketing	Purchasing	Warehouse	Accounting	Accounting
Requisition	Order	Receipt	Invoice	Payment

Often this work depends on a computer system to store and process the data. If all of this goes according to plan then the process is working well. However, as can be seen the process is dependent on people in different functions who will need to liaise with each other if changes occur. What happens if the quantity delivered is not what was ordered? Should the warehouse accept the delivery or send it back? If the quality is not acceptable, who should be informed and how? What level of tolerance, if any, is permitted on the invoice? How many of these business rules are understood by all concerned and which of these are programmed into the computer system?

Some organisations have responded to this need by mapping their key cross-functional processes and by appointing process owners with accountability for the successful design and execution of these processes. However, this is not a straightforward role if the resources remain with the functional heads. If there are no process owners, the IT or business change department needs to take a view on how they will acquire the skills and the organisational support to take a business process view of the organisation.

Business process design – current and future

There are several techniques to analyse how work is performed and currently no standard one is used by every organisation. Some examples of techniques follow. It is advisable for organisations to select appropriate techniques for the situations they wish to analyse and where feasible to use these consistently throughout the organisation. Using a standard format allows analysts, designers and business staff to communicate more easily with each other. The process map below is based upon the 'swimlane' approach, so-called because of the swimming pool look of the chart. It may group activities or tasks by roles, resources or organisational units. We can convert the previous process example into a swimlane view, as shown in Figure 5.2, which shows tasks by business function.

The business process model above represents the 'purchase order to payment' process with swimlanes for each of the functional areas. In common with many business processes, the activities are performed by multiple business functions. As discussed, hand-offs between these functions can cause communication problems both between people and information systems. These are not shown in this simplified process model.

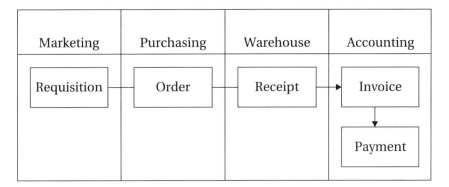

FIGURE 5.2 *Swimlane view of purchasing process*

It is usually the practice to map both the current ('as is') process and the future ('to be') process so as to agree the differences with the stakeholders and plan the business change. The decision on which to start with depends on many factors, such as the nature of the desired change. One option is to start with the 'as is' view if the goal is continuous improvement and the 'to be' view if the goal is radical change where the organisation does not wish to be constrained in the first instance by the current processes. In the revised process shown in Figure 5.3, purchasing sets up a contract for promotional products by which marketing can call-off these goods and make a credit card payment once these have been received.

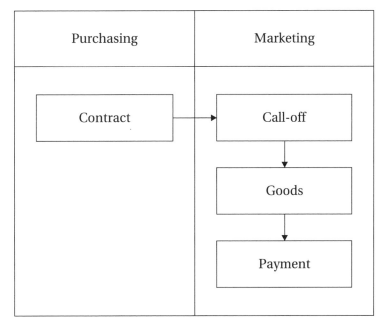

FIGURE 5.3 *Swimlane view of purchasing process – future*

Linking process and people

The swimlane approach can be used to define the tasks performed by a user within a function. Understanding who performs the task and modelling the tasks to be performed enables appropriate jobs to be designed through work practice modelling. Together work practice and task modelling support the design of new processes by analysing how users perform tasks and interact with other users. Activity sampling is a technique that can be used to support work practice and task analysis. This approach involves the collection of data that can then be statistically analysed to determine the amount of time individuals spend on different aspects of their work and to assess the delays between activities. The observations of the activity may be sampled at fixed or random intervals with the choice dependent on the nature of the work. As an extreme example, if an activity was sampled every day at 12.30 p.m., the evaluation may be that the employees are always at lunch.

Linking process and information flows

One method that is suitable to map both process and information flows is called SIPOC, an acronym which extends the input–process–output relationship by considering the key stakeholders, supplier and customer. A **supplier** provides **inputs** to a **process**, which generates **outputs** to a **customer**. The initial letters generate the acronym SIPOC, sometimes reversed as COPIS. It is normal that a high-level process map is initially created consisting of a few key steps. This, for example, might be used to identify the inputs such as material and information from the key suppliers and the outputs such as goods and services provided to the customer. SIPOC is one of the tools of Six Sigma, which is a methodology that uses a data-driven approach to improve quality[14].

INFORMATION

The definition of information and data

One of the challenges of dealing with the topic of information is that it means different things to people depending on their organisational and personal perspective. There are also multiple definitions associated with data and information. Sometimes data is viewed as the raw facts, with one example being numbers presented in isolation. What does the number 56 convey without the context of a category such as age or temperature? Even then more detail may be required such as the temperature scale. Hence information is often viewed as data with meaning. However, it is also the case that many people use the terms 'data' and 'information' interchangeably.

Paradoxically, adding more confusion is the term 'knowledge', which is sometimes viewed as a higher form of information. Knowledge can be explicit, for example, documented in a book or it can be tacit, residing in people's heads. The explicit form is closer to the definition of information, yet there is no universal agreement on the terms. In this chapter, information will be used as the umbrella term. Data is a term often used in an IT context due to its origins in 'data processing', hence there are some terms that will include the word 'data'.

The importance of information management

Information has many roles in supporting business goals and IT-enabled business change. There are different elements of information that support the different goals.

(i)   Transaction data is the term used to describe the information that is collected by and supports the business operations such as purchase orders and purchase invoices.

(ii) Unstructured information is content such as text or pictures stored in documents.

(iii) Master data provides the key facts on business subjects such as suppliers, products and employees that have an ongoing identity in an organisation. For example, a supplier address is a piece of master data that is stored on a supplier master file.

(iv) Information parameters help to define the business rules for a process by holding key data used in the business processes of an organisation such as the credit limit of a customer used in order processing.

(v)   Management information consolidates the transaction data to support tactical decision-making such as the aggregation of orders to identify total sales volume in a month.

(vi) Information flows are the links between functions and business processes such as the number of goods received compared with those ordered, which supports the purchase payment step in a process.

Business information model

The concept of master data is useful in designing information stores since this type of data does not change as frequently as transaction data. It is used to describe business subjects such as suppliers, also known as information entities. Business information models deal with information entities and the relationships between the entities. Figure 5.4 is a simplified example of a business information model where a supplier offers a product for purchase.

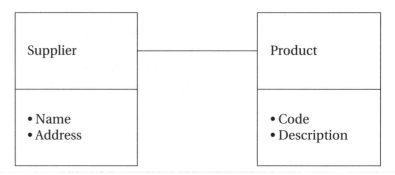

FIGURE 5.4 *Business information model*

The model above shows that the supplier entity has attributes such as name and address while the product entity has attributes such as code and description. There is a relationship between the two entities in that suppliers offer products for sale. The type of relationship can vary. One supplier might offer many products – this is a one-to-many relationship. If multiple suppliers offer a single product there will be a many-to-one relationship. More often both these situations occur forming a many-to-many relationship. Earlier in this chapter we looked at purchasing from a business process perspective. This entity view is from a business information perspective and helps to identify the mainly static data that needs to be recorded in a database. The time and risks in IT-enabled business change increase if the data does not already exist in the organisation systems and must be designed, captured and validated.

Information analysis

In analysing information requirements we need to assess what type of information is needed and by whom. Information is typically required at three different levels in organisations: the strategic, tactical and operational levels. Information is also required to support the particular needs of the various functions within organisations such as production, finance and sales.

Information flows both across the organisation and up and down. The data collected at the operational level mostly comes from the transaction systems. It may be aggregated into a consolidation system or data warehouse which can support planning and reporting at the tactical level. Much of the information that is collected and used at the strategic level is a combination of the internal consolidated data and information that is generated from external sources such as data on economic trends. These different requirements are represented in Figure 5.5. Taking one example in a call centre, the pay of employees can be aggregated to calculate the average monthly costs per employee and

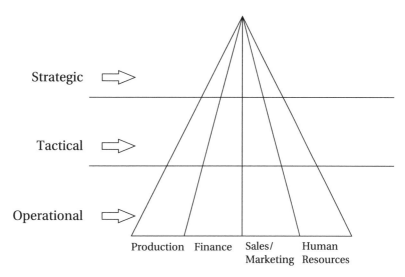

FIGURE 5.5   *Information analysis*

strategic comparisons can be made with long-term cost trends in other countries.

EXERCISE

Construct the information needs at strategic, tactical and operational levels at an organisation that you know or work for. Do this for one function (e.g. finance).

Managing information

The Information Management Model is a conceptual view that was developed with the Information Management Profession (IMP) group[15]. Key contributors were Steve Farquharson, group director of information management at the Metropolitan Police Service, and Mike Fishwick, head of customer information at Yell.

Information can be categorised as structured or unstructured, although in practice some of the latter types may be semi-structured. **Structured** data includes, for example, financial numbers such as price or sales revenue that will normally be held in a fixed format. Examples of **unstructured** data include a free format address or a picture. Information needs to be **controlled**, for example it must be secure and legally compliant. It also needs to be **exploited** by analysing and using it for organisational advantage. These dimensions are shown in Figure 5.6.

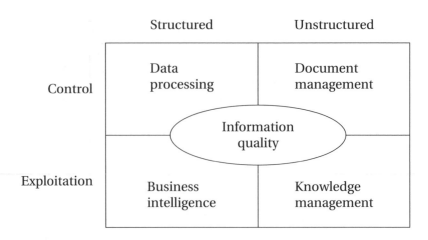

FIGURE 5.6 *Information management model*

The contents of the quadrants are terms that have typically – although not exclusively – been linked to different technologies. These include the following.

- Data processing – this term originates from the early days of computing and describes the processing and control of structured data.
- Document management – the term also extends to records management and content management and relates to the control of unstructured data.
- Business intelligence – this largely relates to the consolidation and analysis of structured data.
- Knowledge management – the process of sharing knowledge – some that is written down (explicit) and some that is in our heads (tacit).
- Information quality – this element ensures that the information contained in all four quadrants is fit for purpose.

The design of business processes and information provides an important link to the design and acquisition of both applications and IT infrastructure components. An application is a specific system to support a business process while the IT infrastructure is a technology platform on which individual applications run. In the design phase it is important to also consider how these applications and infrastructure components are implemented and integrated to provide ongoing services to the business.

TECHNOLOGY

Application and development life cycles

Organisations know that their IT hardware infrastructure, with items such as large computers, is an asset in financial terms and requires maintenance.

There is now increasing recognition that IT applications are also valuable assets for an organisation that need to be managed. Similarities exist with a machine that is used to create volume products; over time it will become obsolescent or need maintenance and replacement (unless it is discarded because the requirement has disappeared). Similarly an application will be used to generate a large number of business transactions based on defined business rules. When these business rules and the technologies change, the application needs to be updated.

Application life cycle management is the approach taken to manage the different stages from the initial requirement to the monitoring of the application and eventually the end of the application use. This includes the requirement definition, development or acquisition of the application, its customisation and integration, delivery and support through to decommissioning.

Application software may be developed or acquired. As highlighted earlier, ERP is a widely used type of application software acquired by organisations. ERP systems offer an integrated solution that was seen as a response to systems developed in an isolated way for each function. Its primary function is to support end-to-end operational business processes by providing applications that process data within and across business functions such as finance, logistics and sales. There has been a consolidation in the ERP marketplace over the last few years. Oracle has chosen to challenge SAP's position as the global leader by acquiring PeopleSoft, who had previously acquired JD Edwards.

The application development life cycle focuses on the stages required to develop rather than purchase an application. Typical stages include analysis, design, build, test and implement (with maintenance recognised as being a key element of ongoing development). In the next chapter there is a review of development and procurement approaches.

Components of a technical design

In today's environment there are very few 'green field' situations where there is no existing IT infrastructure. Therefore, the challenge is to create a design that determines how components will fit into and enhance the current services.

The previous section highlighted that some applications are purchased and some are developed. There is also the option of an application which is a mix of purchased and developed software. This mix typically adds a level of complexity as does the situation where individual applications are purchased from different suppliers. How all these applications fit together is part of the applications architecture and major new applications should be evaluated partly on the impact they have on the target architecture.

Most organisations rarely develop new technologies. They are not usually in the business of developing commodity technologies such as personal computers and telecommunications devices. These will typically be purchased from an established supplier on the basis of factors such as cost, quality and service.

Some organisations are at the front-end of technological innovation. They will have a team that is actively engaged in learning about and trying to apply new and emerging technologies. It can be a difficult balance to stay at the forefront and at the same time be realistic about which new technologies can be applied for real business advantage.

As with the application components, it is important to consider how the IT infrastructure components will fit together as part of the architecture.

Planning the new services

Designing and delivering the application and infrastructure components of a solution is a challenging task. It is a necessary but not sufficient element of the technology part of the solution which needs to be embedded as part of the operational services.

The project management team needs to recognise the service management team as a key stakeholder and engage the different members of this team relatively early in the process (and certainly not wait until the team is just about to implement the new solution).

There will be several points that the project team will wish to discuss with the service management team including reliability, availability, response times, security and disaster recovery. These areas are known as the non-functional requirements (not a particularly descriptive term) due to the fact that they are not perceived to directly impact the business process functionality of the system.

PROGRAMME DESIGN

The previous chapter emphasised the importance of programme management. There are many considerations involved in creating a programme design which encompasses the overall planning for the different deliverables of the IT-enabled business change design.

Defining the programme

In the alignment stage the strategic analysis determines the order of magnitude of the changes required. This will clarify whether there is a need for one or more programmes and projects. As a result of the definition of the business improvement the scope becomes firmer and the decision may be taken to manage the range of deliverables as a programme. Take the NHS system change as an example, which is part of a multi-billion pound programme.

NATIONAL HEALTH SERVICE (NHS) SYSTEM

The United Kingdom NHS IT programme is one of the most ambitious ever attempted for a health service. It aims to link, in a single system, 117,000 doctors, 397,500 nurses, 128,000 scientists and therapists and about 300 hospitals by 2012. It has four key elements. The 'Choose and Book' is a system that should allow patients to make hospital appointments at a time that suits them. A centralised medical record system will hold records for 50 million patients. There will be a facility to provide electronic prescriptions. Fast network links will be available between NHS organisations.

Source: *Daily Telegraph*, 19 June 2006

POINT TO PONDER

What are the characteristics of these deliverables? Which are business-focused and which appear to be more IT focused?

The business case from the improvement phase will outline the key deliverables and should also specify the governance structure. As a minimum it should define the sponsorship and the management structure and roles as defined in the alignment chapter.

Planning the programme

A large programme will be structured as a series of interdependent projects or work streams. One option is that each major deliverable becomes a project. Alternatively there may be separate work streams such as business process, IT and change management. Whichever route is chosen, there will need to be individual plans that are then consolidated into an overall plan for the programme.

As with any well-planned project, there should be an explicit resource allocation which will cover both internal and external people. It is good practice to cost internal resources in addition to external resources. This ensures a more accurate representation of costs and makes it easier to substitute external for internal resources if there are conflicting priorities.

There will be several groups involved in planning the programme. These include the programme manager and the project managers who plan the delivery. Business change managers will plan the transition into the business operational environment. A key enabler of a successful programme is a programme office to support the planning and tracking of the programme.

Programme stream interdependencies

Most large IT-enabled business change programmes require each of the elements covered in this chapter. This results in a requirement for professional and experienced designers for the organisation and people elements, the business process and information models and also the applications and technology designs. Supported by this expertise the programme manager can take the broad requirements identified during the alignment phase and develop a more detailed view of the solution for the implementation phase. In a small project, there might be a single person who has to fulfil multiple roles.

One major challenge is to ensure that the design is an integrated one. For example, if the process and information models are created independently by different projects or streams, the programme manager needs to ensure that these are consistent. An appropriate methodology will help to address this issue and this is therefore a key design decision for an IT-enabled change programme.

CASE STUDY QUESTIONS

Review the case study on Foods. First you should gain an overview of the case (if not already done) and then focus in particular on the business change design stage. What were the main components of the programme? How were these components integrated? What management approach was taken to the programme?

SUMMARY

The chapter has covered the third stage of the IT-enabled business change life cycle. This stage of designing the business change links the definition of the improvement to the implementation phase. As articulated, this is much more than a specification of an IT system and the broad range of skills required for successful design is a challenge for most organisations. We have broadly covered the following topics.

TOPICS: BUSINESS CHANGE DESIGN

There are many elements that form an IT-enabled business change. This chapter takes the main areas in turn, examines their main components and shows how the various elements interrelate. It looks at the organisational and people aspects as well as the IT involved. It covers:

- Aspects of organisational change:
  - the organisation structure including boundaries and relationships;
  - the principles of performance measurement;
  - the identification of key attributes of the organisational culture.

- Aspects of people change:
  - ✦ understanding the differences between jobs and roles;
  - ✦ the identification of training needs;
  - ✦ the importance of motivation and reward.

- Aspects of process change:
  - ✦ the difference between a function and a business process;
  - ✦ the features of current ('as is') business processes;
  - ✦ the features of future ('to be') business processes.
- Information management:
  - ✦ the definition of information management;
  - ✦ the elements of information management;
  - ✦ the importance of information management in the delivery of business change.
- Applications and technology services:
  - ✦ the application and development life cycles;
  - ✦ the components of a technical design;
  - ✦ planning the new services.
- Programme design:
  - ✦ the definition of a programme for business change;
  - ✦ the need to plan a programme;
  - ✦ the importance of planning for the interdependencies of organisation, people, process, information and technology streams.

SAMPLE QUESTIONS

Question 20

All individual processes on a business process model, should:

(a) describe detailed business rules;
(b) add value to the overall process;
(c) cross-reference processes to data;
(d) relate to all other processes.

Discussion

Processes will have different characteristics depending on the level at which they are described. At certain levels they may describe business rules and cross-reference to data. They may relate to other processes; however, this is not mandatory. They should always add value to the overall process.

Question 21

Which of the following best describes the purpose of a business process model?

(a) To show the tasks done within a functional area.
(b) To demonstrate the business process for an item of software.
(c) To show the sequence of tasks across a process.
(d) To show the detailed business rules within a process.

Discussion

A process model reviews the sequence of tasks across a process which may span more than one functional area. It does not have to be related to software or show the detailed business rules.

Question 22

Which of the following are examples of unstructured information?

(i) Email content.
(ii) Relational database record.
(iii) Graphic of a company's logo.
(iv) Legal document.

(a) i, iii, iv.
(b) ii, iii, iv.
(c) i, ii, iii.
(d) i, ii, v.

Discussion

The only information that will be held in a structured format is that within a relational database record hence (a) is the correct answer. This question highlights that unstructured information is not held only in text format. There may be other formats such as graphics and voice.

Question 23

Which of the following are elements of the Soft Systems Methodology CATWOE technique?

 (i) Actors.
 (ii) Environment.
 (iii) Trainers.
 (iv) Owners.

 (a) i, iii, iv.
 (b) ii, iii, iv.
 (c) i, ii, iii.
 (d) i, ii, iv.

Discussion

This is a straightforward question if you are familiar with the CATWOE acronym. The T stands for transformation hence (d) is the correct answer.

Question 24

Which of the following lists contains **only** non-functional requirements?

 (a) Archiving, screen contents, robustness.
 (b) Response time, security, availability.
 (c) Business rules, accuracy, capacity.
 (d) Access rights, back-up levels, data validation.

Discussion

Screen contents, business rules and data validation are examples of functional requirements that always relate to the specific business area, hence (b) is the correct answer.

Question 25

Which software type is most suitable for creating end-to-end operational processes?

 (a) Mobile data capture systems.
 (b) Enterprise resource planning (ERP).
 (c) Business intelligence.
 (d) Data warehouse.

Discussion

An ERP is the most suitable software type to create an end-to-end process such as: receive a customer order, deliver the goods, invoice the customer and collect the cash. The other software types typically operate more at the front-end, such as mobile capture, or the back-end, such as data warehouse and business intelligence.

Question 26

Which of the following would you **not** expect to see as an output in a business change definition?

    (a) Applications design.
    (b) Description of the 'to be' process.
    (c) Documented business strategy.
    (d) Training requirements.

Discussion

All of the above may be an output apart from the documented business strategy, which should already have been produced before this stage of the IT-enabled business change life cycle.

Question 27

Which of the following best describes the term 'Information'?

    (a) Information is data organised and presented in a meaningful manner.
    (b) Information is another word for data.
    (c) Information is the name for any data that is held in an information system.
    (d) Information is any data that is properly obtained, collected and stored.

Discussion

Information is more than just data held in a computer or manual system. It is data organised to provide meaning. While it might be based on data that is properly obtained, collected and stored, this may not always be the case.

Question 28

What is the primary capability provided by an ERP package?

    (a) It supports and links business functions with consistent data.
    (b) It manages relationships with customers and suppliers.
    (c) It provides tools to plan the finances of the enterprise.
    (d) It is a management information source for senior executives.

Discussion

An ERP package performs many individual tasks which may help finance, customer relationships and management information. However, its primary capability is to support integrated enterprise processes with consistent data.

6 Change Implementation

'There are no IT projects, only business projects – remembering this is essential to the successful delivery and implementation of projects.'

Paul Coby, CIO, British Airways

INTRODUCTION AND PLANNING OF THE CHANGE

The implementation stage of the business change life cycle is concerned with the execution of the integrated changes within the organisation. The deliverables from this stage are the implemented changes, which may include a new or enhanced IT system, revised business processes, re-trained staff, new information reports and revised management structures. The successful implementation of the change programme will be dependent upon careful change management. This is required particularly to co-ordinate all of the different elements of the change programme, including taking account of the culture of the organisation and the affected stakeholders.

The introduction of the business change is where the programme and the operational teams must work closely together to ensure that the implementation is effective. This requires a structured approach to accepting, deploying and gaining buy-in to the solution, hence implementation will need to be planned carefully. Once the solution has been acquired, either through purchase or development or a mix, it needs to be deployed. This requires a buy-in to the solution from the receivers of change. After being deployed, a post implementation review (PIR) should take place, as shown in Figure 6.1.

FIGURE 6.1 *Process and systems transition life cycle*

The selected approach to implementing the plan will depend partly on the degree of change and deciding whether this should be evolutionary or revolutionary. Common approaches to implementing IT-enabled business change are big bang versus incremental. The former is where all the functions are implemented at the same time, while the latter implements the functionality over several time periods or phases. This is a critical choice and not always an easy one given the many factors involved in the decision.

EXERCISE

You have been asked to introduce a new standard accounting system across three geographical business units to replace different national systems. Additionally you need to provide a consolidated reporting system for the head office of the organisation which will take accounting data from each of the business unit systems. The national business units and the head office require both statutory and management reports.

What options are there for an incremental approach? What are the pros and cons of a big bang versus an incremental approach?

The implementation plan will also be influenced by how the solution is to be acquired. Initially this will be a choice between buy and build. The buy option will require strong engagement with the supplier(s) in the creation of a realistic plan. If the build option is selected then there is a further choice to developing the solution between linear and iterative approaches. These options impact the plan and are explored in more detail in this chapter.

ACQUIRING THE SOLUTION

A key decision in planning the implementation is to determine whether the components of the solution should be purchased or developed.

Purchasing solution components

An application that is purchased is sometimes known as an 'off-the-shelf' package or 'commercial off-the-shelf' (COTS) packages. The methodology for a COTS package is different from that of an in-house development since the aim is ideally to match the software functionality to the business process without modification of the program code. Flexible COTS packages have a large number of parameters that can be set to satisfy the specific business rules of an organisation.

Although organisations start with the intention of having no in-house development, many have found that the purchased application package does not fit the business sufficiently well. Hence, in practice many applications that are bought need some degree of customisation of the program code to fit the business process.

Development approaches

If the decision has been taken to develop a system, choices remain about how this development will be done. The two main options are to take a linear, sequential approach or to adopt an evolutionary iterative approach. An example of the former is SSADM (Structured Systems

Analysis and Design Method) while a RAD (Rapid Application Development) approach is indicative of the latter.

Whichever approach is taken, there is still the need to go through the stages of analysis, design, build, test and implement. In a linear sequential approach the assumption is that each phase is carried out once and there is no going back. This is why a common term for this approach is a 'waterfall' methodology since the water goes one way. One of the main concerns expressed with linear methods is that the user sees the result only at the end and by this time changes may have occurred or misunderstandings been built into the system.

Generally a structured approach is more appropriate when the requirements are clear and the technology is proven while an iterative approach is preferred when there is uncertainty about the requirements or the technology is new. Building a prototype is one method of iteration. For example, an application that shows only the flow between the input and output screens can be easy to construct and it will help users to visualise the system as it was before major investments in technology and resources.

SSADM and RAD are labels for methodology approaches that have been in use for many years. This is an evolving field. For example, DSDM (Dynamic Systems Development Method) is a framework that formalises the iterative approach focusing on strong user involvement and incremental delivery. More recently the term Agile has been applied to methods that are based on an adaptive iterative approach rather than a plan-based view. Combining DSDM and Agile project management is DSDM Atern, which can be accessed via the website. www.DSDM.org

More information on development methods is available on a number of websites including that of OGC[16].

DEPLOYING THE SOLUTION

Deployment represents the transition from being a change project to providing an operational service. It is sometimes regarded as the 'moment of truth'? This type of phrase suggests a one-off evaluation of success. It is true to say that there may be some specific measures such as the system technically working or a key reconciliation test being met. In practice, though, successful deployment requires a number of elements to be managed individually and together over a period of time. The technology not only needs to work, it must also have the right performance, reliability, scalability and security. Some of these features may be observable quickly; others may not be apparent for some time.

Information is one component that is typically key to the deployment but which it may not be possible to evaluate immediately. Some major systems implementations have suffered from poor migration of data from the old to the new systems. It is advisable to plan the data migration early in the process and to devise methods for assessing the quality of the data.

The fact that deployment connects the project to the operational service also highlights the importance of a constructive collaboration between the project and service teams and between the business and the IT participants. As an example of these links, testing the IT-enabled business change requires co-operation between the delivery team and those accepting that the solution works.

Agreeing, conducting and accepting tests are vital parts of the deployment process. Both system testers and business process testers must ensure that the planning, design, management, execution and reporting of tests are appropriately executed. They will, however, have different focuses. The system testers will need to be sure that the systems perform as specified including any interfaces to existing and external systems. In contrast the business process testers will need to ensure that a realistic and comprehensive set of scenarios have been formulated that test both the functionality and the usability of the new process.

In the SFIA model, the systems tests are part of the IT systems development category whereas the business process tests are part of the business change category. There is a corresponding link in the area of change management. It is sometimes a source of confusion in the area of IT-enabled business change that the IT and change management professionals use the term 'change management' to mean different things. In the IT world, and most noticeably in the ITIL (IT Infrastructure Library) community, the term 'change management' refers to the changes in the IT infrastructure covering the request for change through to successful implementation in a controlled way that ensures no disruption to the live services. In contrast the human resources community use 'change management' to mean the process of introducing the change into business operations and in particular gaining the buy-in of people to the change, which is covered in the next section.

ENSURING BUY-IN TO THE SOLUTION

When an organisation embarks on change it wants the transition to be as smooth as possible and for the change to be fully implemented rather than risking having to regress to the previous state. An understanding of how people react to change is necessary to ensure buy-in to the solution. Lewin's model deals with preparing for the transition and reinforcing the change[17]. This has three states:

(i) Unfreezing: in this period, existing attitudes and beliefs are 'unfrozen' in preparation for the proposed change.

(ii) Transition: the movement from the previous to the new way of working.

(iii) Refreezing: this is the phase where changes are institutionalised and the organisation 'refrozen' in the new configuration.

POINT TO PONDER

Reflect on what types of communications need to be planned in each of the three phases.

One of the techniques used to analyse the positive and negative forces for change is force field analysis. Force field analysis provides a framework for looking at the factors (described as forces) that influence any given situation. It looks at forces that are either driving movement toward a goal (helping forces) or blocking movement toward a goal (hindering forces). It is particularly useful to understand these positive and negative forces in dealing with the unfreezing stage of an organisation.

Acceptance of change

Implementing any new process or system involves a period of transition from the existing state to the new state. There are many reasons why this transition reflects an initial dip in performance before improved organisational benefits are realised. One cause for a drop and then an increase in productivity is a **learning curve effect** as people adapt to the new systems. Another is a **progress effect** as implementation issues

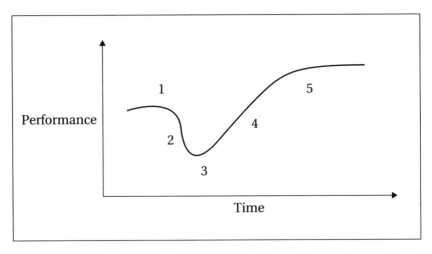

FIGURE **6.2** *Performance change curves, adapted from Schein (1965) and Carnall (1999)*

arising from poor quality are resolved. There is also a **psychological effect in coping** with the effects of a change that is linked to the other effects. A personal coping cycle that encompasses five stages has the acronym SARAH, which represents shock, anger, rejection, acceptance and hope.

It is important for those planning a significant change to be aware of the potential impacts so that they can aim to minimise the effects and also so that they can manage the expectations of key stakeholders. In order to plan and monitor a process and systems change, it is helpful to consider the different stages that may occur. There is no consistent view on the terminology across the three types of effects; however, many models encompass variations of the five stages shown in Figure 6.2.

Stage 1 is when the change is launched. It needs a strong communications effort to support the new business process, which will typically be received differently by people with some adopting a 'wait and see' attitude and others concerned by the prospect of change.

As the change is implemented in stage 2 people see the problems and lose a degree of confidence in both the systems and other people who are finding it difficult to adapt to the change. This is where a prior focus on quality (system, information, service) can help to reduce the breadth and depth of the dip in performance.

Stage 3 represents the low point in performance but also a turning point as people start to become familiar with the new process and how best to use the features of the new system.

The overall performance increases in stage 4 as individual and organisational productivity increases.

Finally, in stage 5, performance levels out, ideally at a much higher level than before the change.

There are some key points to take away from these transition models:

- People will display a range of emotions throughout the change and will need varying degrees of support – this may involve extra training, talking issues through with someone, getting involved in the change or just being allowed to have their say.
- It is important to try to minimise the negative stages and build on the positive stages through proactive change management. This includes having a robust project plan, a consistent communications plan, investment in training and good user support during and after system implementation.
- The communications plan needs to build on the stakeholder analysis by identifying key concerns, targeting these through tailored messages which are delivered through the appropriate channels and then monitoring the feedback.

EXERCISE

Think of a time when an organisation you were involved in went though a significant change which transformed the way it operated and required you to undergo new learning and form new relationships.

What were the forces that helped or hindered the change?

Describe the change using the types of effects identified above. What was the strongest effect?

Were any of these not present and, if not, can you explain why not?

Culture

The approaches to managing the transition and the shape of the transition curve are likely to vary depending on the organisation and national cultures as described earlier. An organisation which has a power culture may be very committed to communications but this is likely to be one-way messages from the top, whereas a person culture is more likely to engage people in the change. There may be practical reasons why these cultures have emerged over time. A high security factory will have strong processes and controls with little room for debate, in contrast to a medium-sized knowledge management consultancy which may be keen to demonstrate that it follows its own advice.

In a similar way, the national culture can influence the way that the change is communicated throughout the organisation. A multinational organisation may have an underlying power culture but if the change is communicated in a country that has a low power distance there is likely to be more debate about the change. Of course more debate does not mean that the change will not be accepted and neither does less debate mean that the change will categorically be welcomed.

Managers who operate for a long time in a multinational environment have learned not to take the first response as a definite indicator of action. It is advisable to take advice from someone who understands the national culture when interpreting a response in a sensitive situation.

REVIEWING THE IMPLEMENTATION

The sponsor and programme manager should organise a PIR following the implementation of the change. A PIR is a formal review of a programme or project. It is used to answer the question: did we achieve what we set out to do, in business terms, and if not, what should be done?

A PIR is typically done when there has been time to demonstrate the learning or business benefits of an IT-enabled change programme. Some organisations will conduct these reviews of learning and benefits at different times depending on the type of change that has occurred. There may also be a third type of review which is conducted within a month or so after the implementation and focuses very much on whether the solution is working as planned independently of the learning points and the benefits. This is very much a reactive review to address any issues that remain as a result of the implementation and that were not resolved within a short period after the implementation. Depending on the severity of the issues, action teams may be formed to focus resources on the known problems. If the IT-enabled change is a major one, it is advisable to plan-in a period of stabilisation before disbanding the project teams.

Similarly, for a major programme of change there may be several PIRs over time – a programme of business change may take years to complete and the business system it supports may be in existence for an even longer period of time. The level of cost, risk and benefit delivered by the change must be reviewed periodically, following the first PIR. It may be appropriate to conduct tailored PIRs after the full PIR, to address only those key areas that reflect current business priorities.

As discussed earlier, there are both 'hard' and 'soft' elements of the change with methodology and communications being examples of these two types. It is important that both of these contributors to the change are explored in the PIR. The learning points and responses are likely to be different in these cases.

It follows that for reviews to be effective they must be conducted in an open and constructive manner with participants ready to make and receive constructive criticism. This is vital if applicable lessons are to be learned and appropriate actions taken. The PIR is not intended to redesign the whole change programme although it may suggest improvements to each of the components, including processes, information, skills and technology.

A PIR is an essential component of the benefits management process, which is reviewed in the next chapter. In summary, it checks whether benefits, including those set out in the business case, have been achieved and identifies opportunities for further improvement.

CASE STUDY QUESTIONS

Review the case study on Foods. First you should gain an overview of the case (if not already done) and then focus in particular on the implementation stage. What were the key choices made in the implementation stage? How did the team ensure buy-in from the stakeholders? What post-implementation reviews took place and what were the outcomes?

SUMMARY

This chapter has covered the fourth stage of the IT-enabled business change life cycle. This stage of implementation determines whether the programme will work or not. Decisions on this stage need to be made earlier in the process to articulate and manage the risks. If successful it provides a very good platform for generating the benefits. We have broadly covered the following topics.

TOPICS: BUSINESS CHANGE IMPLEMENTATION

In this chapter the reader learns about the processes that should be employed in the introduction of IT-enabled business change. Taking each in turn, it covers the entire life cycle from inception to implementation to final review. The topics include:

- Planning the implementation:
    - ✦ place of planning in the business change life cycle;
    - ✦ deciding the approach to accepting the solution;
    - ✦ deciding the approach to deploying the solution;
    - ✦ deciding the approach to ensuring buy-in of the solution.
- Acquiring the solution:
    - ✦ place of acquisition in the business change life cycle;
    - ✦ development approaches;
    - ✦ procurement approaches;
    - ✦ the importance of documentation.
- Deploying the solution:
    - ✦ place of deployment in the business change life cycle;
    - ✦ roles required to deploy business change;
    - ✦ managing the change to avoid disruption.
- Ensuring buy-in to the solution:
    - ✦ place of ensuring buy-in in the business change life cycle;
    - ✦ stakeholder acceptance of change;
    - ✦ organisational culture and national culture.

- Reviewing the change implementation:
  - ✦ place of review in the business change life cycle;
  - ✦ assessing the solution;
  - ✦ monitoring progress and measuring success via production of a post-implementation review;
  - ✦ lessons learnt.

SAMPLE QUESTIONS

Question 29

The term PIR stands for:

  (a) post implementation review;
  (b) post initiation review;
  (c) project initiation report;
  (d) programme implementation report.

Discussion

This is a straightforward question if you are familiar with the PIR acronym. The correct answer is (a) as the aim is to identify lessons conducted from a post implementation review at the end of the IT-enabled change programme.

Question 30

Which of the following is **not** a main source of documented information needed to do a formal review once implementation has taken place?

  (a) The business case.
  (b) Previous similar reviews.
  (c) Stakeholder analysis.
  (d) A summary of costs and benefits.

Discussion

A formal review after implementation will evaluate the costs and benefits against the business case, taking into account previous reviews. While stakeholders will be consulted during this review, a prior stakeholder analysis is not a main source of documented information.

Question 31

Force field analysis provides a way of identifying:

  (a) a mechanism for driving change across organisational boundaries in situations that show resistance;
  (b) where the change is most likely to provide the greatest value within an organisation;
  (c) where effort will be required in helping change and overcoming resistance to it;
  (d) a set of steps that will help to force through change.

Discussion

Force field analysis does not provide the answers or the benefits in driving through change. What it does do is identify where effort will be required in helping change and overcoming resistance to it.

Question 32

Which of the following statements does **not** define the need for a contract?

    (a) To specify a clear timing on project phases and deliverables.
    (b) To convince the customer of the reasons to set the project up.
    (c) To identify the roles involved in the process and their duties.
    (d) To establish a clear set of conditions in a customer/supplier relationship.

Discussion

A contract should be clear on timing, roles and terms and conditions. The rationale for setting up the project should have been identified in a prior phase.

Question 33

Which of the following activities do **not** form part of the 'unfreezing' phase of a change?

    (a) Ensuring restraining forces do not regain their former influences.
    (b) Involvement of staff in planning and preparation for change.
    (c) Identifying and addressing resistance to change.
    (d) Development of publicity campaigns to enforce key messages.

Discussion

The unfreeze phase is the first of the change phases. Identifying restraining forces and providing effective communications to stakeholders is important in this phase. Ensuring that restraining forces do not regain their former influences is a task for a later phase.

Question 34

Which role in the implementation of business change is responsible for translating high-level business plans into formal business cases and ensuring that these remain visible throughout?

    (a) Programme management.
    (b) Quality management.
    (c) Business change management.
    (d) Supplier management.

Discussion

Different members of the team will contribute to the business case; however, the development of the business case from the high-level business plans is the responsibility of the programme manager.

Question 35

What should the business sponsor **not** be directly managing during the implementation phase?

   (a) Technology solution works according to the specification.
   (b) Negative impacts on the receivers of the change.
   (c) Risks that the benefits will not be achieved.
   (d) Confidence of top management in the planned change.

Discussion

The sponsor needs to focus on the benefits and the risks working closely with key stakeholders. It is not the responsibility (or the likely skills profile) of the sponsor to manage the technology solution delivery.

7 Benefits Management

Measuring benefits is essential but it is equally important to keep reviewing the quality and efficiency of delivery of those benefits.

Peter Ford, resources director, executive board member,
Chelsea Building Society

WHY BENEFITS MANAGEMENT?

Many business change projects fail to deliver the benefits on which the investment was originally justified. Some surveys suggest that 30–40% of systems to support business change deliver no benefits whatsoever. The ongoing costs will usually be monitored – but the anticipated benefits are not so easy to quantify and track. Benefits management ensures that business change achieves the expected results by translating business objectives into measurable benefits that can be systematically tracked. This chapter examines the types of benefits and how these relate to financial measures. It considers non-financial benefits linked to a balanced scorecard approach. Measurement of benefits is supported through key performance indicators and strategy. Finally there is a life cycle view of benefits realisation.

TYPES OF BENEFITS

Predicting and evaluating business benefits are challenging tasks. They are critical to establishing a justification for the typically large investments that are made in IT-enabled change. There is a distinction between a **feature**, which represents an element of functionality supporting the change, and a **benefit**, which relates to the outcome of the change. Being able to offer self-service through an e-business application may be a new capability; however, it only becomes a benefit if, for example, it increases the level of sales or satisfaction.

A starting point is to consider whether a positive outcome leads to a financial or non-financial benefit. Examples of financial benefits arising are changes that reduce spend either in relation to existing costs or by avoiding expenditure. Alternatively the benefit may be one of increased income. The net financial benefit is a consolidated outcome of these two flows. Replacing sales staff with an automated ordering system might reduce costs but if the contribution from sales revenue decreases by a larger amount, the result will be declining profitability. This reinforces the need for a holistic view of IT-enabled business change.

Some benefits are not easily translated into financial terms. An investment in developing communication skills in an organisation is unlikely to have a direct impact on the financial bottom line. If, however, it helps to improve the success rate of business change, there will be a visible positive impact.

A cumulative categorisation of benefits (Ward and Peppard 2002) is shown below.

- Observable.
- Measurable.
- Quantifiable.
- Financial.

This list is a hierarchy of benefit categories. A benefit first needs to be capable of being observed in some way; for example, can we establish that customers are more satisfied as a result of an IT-enabled business change through fewer complaints to the call centre.

The next step is assessing if the benefit is capable of being measured; for example, satisfaction may be measured through a pre-planned questionnaire or interview and compared with a position existing before the IT-enabled business change.

If the benefit can be measured, the result might be qualitative or quantifiable. Customers who give positive comments in an interview might confirm a measurable but not necessarily quantifiable change. Alternatively there may be data available from a survey such as 80% of the customers are happy with the response time on calls made to the customer service centre compared with 60% before the change.

Finally in this case the question is whether the degree of customer satisfaction can legitimately be translated into a financial benefit. For example, is there a defined relationship between satisfaction and increased revenue? Do the people who are happy with the response times place more or higher-value orders.

Relationship to accounting

If a direct financial benefit exists, it should be possible to identify where this benefit will materialise in the organisation's financial and management accounts. There are, for example, key categories of costs in these financial accounts such as the profit and loss statement in a commercial organisation. In the case where there is a reduction in salary costs, this should show as an increase in profitability in the financial accounts. However, there may be an initial restructuring cost, which means that the savings will not materialise until the second year.

Another example is a new logistics system that introduces improved algorithms providing the same level of customer service with a lower average stock. The resulting financial benefit of reduced value of stock may be linked to the level of interest to be paid for these stocks. This will be reflected in a reduction in the value of current assets in the financial accounts. If the lower level of stock means that there is no need to purchase an existing warehouse there will be a cost avoidance impact with a lower projected fixed asset level.

Engaging the finance department will ensure that the costs and benefits are appropriately represented in the business case. Policies such as defining over what period to depreciate the assets are not the same in every organisation. The finance director in an organisation may also have strong views that projected benefits should be confirmed by adjusting future budgets to reflect the revenue or saving opportunity. It is advisable to engage with the finance director or their representative early in the process of defining benefits.

FINANCIAL BENEFITS AND INVESTMENT APPRAISAL

Financial benefits are the key contributor to the ROI. The ROI for a business change calculates the net benefits by subtracting the costs incurred from the gross benefits. This is the effective ROI. Financial benefits will arise from either an increase in the income of an organisation or a decrease in the costs. Few investments in business change can be solely linked to an increase in income. One example that is more attributable than others is where existing products are later sold on the internet with no increase in advertising. Revenue from this new channel can be more directly linked to the business change.

A decrease in costs may occur through reduced operating expenses such as material or labour costs. Lower stockholding levels result in

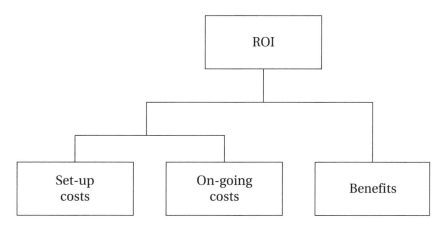

FIGURE 7.1   *Costs and benefits*

reduced costs (due to interest costs or opportunity cost through released space) and there may be opportunities to avoid investment in fixed assets such as factories or equipment. As with the cost analysis, the benefits from reduced costs need to take account of whether these are one-off or ongoing costs. Headcount savings that are sustainable will normally be treated as an ongoing saving since this reduces the annual salary bill on a yearly basis. The benefits need to be matched to the costs as shown in Figure 7.1.

The financial benefits are offset by the set-up costs and the ongoing costs to give the projected net benefits from the IT-enabled business change. An investment is justified in financial terms if the net benefits are positive and the value meets the criteria set by the organisation. There are several metrics that may be used by organisations, as illustrated in Table 7.1 and below.

Year 0 is assumed to be the point at which the investment is made and the set-up costs are incurred. In years 1 to 4 ongoing costs are incurred and benefits have started to be realised with the assumptions that these both happen at the end of the year. Net benefit represents the benefits minus the costs and the cumulative figure is the cumulative new benefits. All figures are assumed to be cash flows.

TABLE 7.1   *Costs and benefits*

	Costs (£)	Benefits (£)	Net benefit (£)	Cumulative (£)
Year 0	100	0	−100	−100
Year 1	60	80	20	−80
Year 2	40	80	40	−40
Year 3	40	80	40	0
Year 4	40	80	40	40
Total	**280**	**320**	**40**	**40**
ROI%	14.3			

The total cumulative return calculated as the total of benefits minus costs over the period is £40. As a percentage of the total investment this is 40/280, which is about 14%.

Payback

Looking at the timing of the financial costs and benefits will determine how long it takes for the benefits to start to outweigh the costs. This is known as the payback period. The time to pay back the investment is when the cumulative total is zero, hence the simple payback is three years, assuming the costs and the benefits occur at the end of each year.

Discount rate and NPV

More sophisticated methods recognise that economic variables such as inflation and opportunity cost influence the value of income in future time periods. The income in future years therefore needs to be discounted by a factor. In Table 7.1 the discount factor is not shown and is assumed to be 0%, which means that the present value remains at £40.

If we now set the discount rate to a more realistic figure of 7% the net present value reduces to about £16 compared with £40 if the discount factor was set at zero.

Discount rate:	7%
NPV:	£15.70

The discount rate can vary depending on the source of the funds. If the IT investment was financed by a bank borrowing the discount rate would be the interest rate, or in a large organisation it would be the cost of capital of the funds in the business.

Measures

There are different definitions of ROI so it is advisable to understand which financial measures are used in an organisation to evaluate investments. It is also important to investigate what are the target numbers for these financial measures. For example, an organisation might expect an IT-enabled business change investment to have a payback period of less than three years. There is little point in putting forward a proposal that has a payback period of 10 years unless there are other very strong reasons for the investment.

Note: this section on financial benefits and investment appraisal benefited from a review and input from Dr Carole Print, subject area leader, finance, at Henley Management College.

NON-FINANCIAL BENEFITS AND BALANCED SCORECARD

One way a company's performance can be evaluated is by assessing its financial performance using data that is available through its published accounts. A key issue with this approach is that it is largely backward-looking since the financial results relate to previous years. It is possible to extrapolate the financial performance into the future but these projections are largely theoretical without knowing how the company is doing on a range of other measures such as customer satisfaction and business process performance.

A balanced business scorecard addresses some of the issues by capturing both financial and non-financial measures of performance. It is a well-known tool developed by Kaplan and Norton (1996) and is used by many organisations as part of the overall measurement of performance. The balanced scorecard provides a view as to what companies should measure in non-financial areas in order to 'balance' this with the financial perspective.

The balanced scorecard aims to enable organisations to clarify their vision, set targets and translate the strategy into action using appropriate measures and initiatives. In addition to financial results it provides feedback on the customer perspective, the internal business processes and how well the company is doing in promoting learning and growth in order to continuously improve the performance and results. Figure 7.2 presents this perspective.

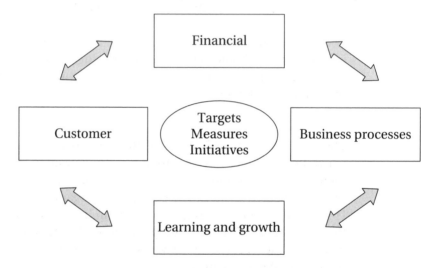

FIGURE 7.2   *Balanced scorecard approach*

The selected measures will vary for each organisation. For example, a logistics company will have customer measures such as the percentage of orders delivered on time. In contrast, one would expect that a call centre company will be keen to measure the average time to answer the phone.

Customer and learning measures are often seen as lead indicators for financial performance. This means that if a large number of customers are unhappy today this is likely to be reflected in the financial performance of tomorrow. In support of this 'common-sense view' a well-known study of a large US retailer found a clear link between employee satisfaction, customer satisfaction and the future financial results. It is not easy to create a quantifiable relationship between these variables; however, they are recognised as critical success factors in many organisations.

BENEFITS MEASUREMENT

Approaches to measuring benefits

The types of benefits have previously been categorised as ranging from observable through measurable and quantified to financial. This has been further expanded with a discussion on financial and non-financial benefits related to the ROI and the balanced scorecard. Next we examine a method of calculating projected benefits which links back to the objectives and strategies of the organisations and derives the KPIs.

KPIs provide the important information that tracks the progress of a selected organisation variable such as the average time it takes to pay invoices. They are quantifiable although sometimes the data are not available for a precise figure. KPIs are most useful in helping to visualise and analyse a trend. They may also be compared to a benchmark figure. For example, an organisation may wish to track how quickly it responds to customer queries in relation to competitors.

EXERCISE

Consider an important activity that you perform. This may be either work-related or linked to a personal situation. What is your KPI and how are you performing against this KPI?

For example, a common health message at this time is that everyone should eat five portions of fruit and vegetables a day. If this is a goal that you agree with, have you identified this as a KPI, and if so, how are you measuring your performance against this KPI? How do you know if the portions you are eating are the right amount? Is it OK to average out over the week? Does it matter which type of fruit or vegetable you eat?

Source: http://www.bbc.co.uk/health/healthy_living/nutrition/basics_fruitveg1.shtml

---

In analysing your own KPIs you may conclude that this is both a powerful technique and one that is not always easy to apply. Of course this depends on the KPI that you have selected. One of the challenges faced by organisations is deciding on which KPIs are appropriate for their particular situation. A technique that can be used to help in generating KPIs is the definition of critical success factors as a linkage between objectives and KPIs.

Critical success factors

Critical success factors (CSF) (Rockart 1979) represent the limited number of areas in which satisfactory results will ensure successful competitive performance. They support the achievement of organisational goals and act as a way of organising and filtering a large amount of data for use by executives and managers. Figure 7.3 offers a structured approach that links KPIs to CSFs within the context of the organisation objectives and overall strategy.

This approach first reviews the objectives of an organisation and links these to the strategies required to achieve the objectives. From this combination are derived the CSFs and the KPIs using the sequence defined in Figure 7.3.

FIGURE 7.3   *CSFs and KPIs*

As an example, a key objective of an organisation might be to reduce costs by 10%. The strategy selected to achieve this objective may be to centralise purchasing. One of the critical success factors for central purchasing might be to achieve discounts while at the same time maintaining the level of on-time deliveries. In this case two KPIs follow, one to measure the discount achieved through central purchasing, the other to measure the on-time deliveries as a percentage of all deliveries and compare this with previous periods. Without setting a KPI for the service-level measure of on-time deliveries the organisation might achieve its cost reduction goals but inadvertently at the expense of internal efficiency and customer satisfaction. It is possible that the organisation might be willing to accept a small drop in performance if the cost reduction is great enough; however, it is still important to be able to measure this drop.

This is one example and there may be many objectives and strategies that map to the critical success factors resulting in a large number of KPIs.

Some of these, as in the case above, may initially be seen as potentially conflicting KPIs such as reducing costs and investing more in brand communications. In this case the answer may be to reduce purchasing cost and release funds which can partly be invested in growing the brand. However, this resolution may not always be possible in which case decisions need to be made on which measures take precedence in given circumstances.

KPIs are potentially a very useful tool in benefits measurement and realisation. If the appropriate KPIs are set up before an IT-enabled change programme is initiated these KPIs can be used to track progress against targets.

BENEFITS MANAGEMENT AND REALISATION

Benefits realisation relies on a process with people that are persistent about achieving the business benefits predicted in the business case. It requires constant attention to business benefits throughout the business change life cycle. Articulation of the benefits in the business case is followed by managing the project in order to deliver the predicted benefits. Once the project has been implemented the need is to check progress on the achievement of the target benefits and take any action required to support their delivery.

It requires a relatively mature organisation to perform effective benefits realisation and this is often the third stage. In the first stage an organisation is able to define the benefits in the business case. In the second stage the organisation performs effective post-implementation reviews of benefits. Benefits ownership and realisation in the third stage then acts as a bridge between the start and end stages of benefits management, as shown in Figure 7.4.

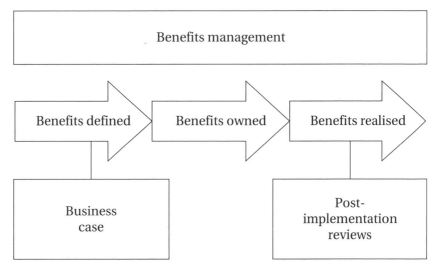

FIGURE 7.4 *Benefits management*

The Office for Government Commerce provides the following definition of benefits management on its website:

> 'Benefits management is the identification of potential benefits, their planning and tracking, the assignment of responsibilities and authorities and their actual realisation as a result of investing in business change.'

The importance of a benefits realisation approach is that it enhances the focus of a well-managed project. In the narrow definition of a project, the goals are to deliver the specified product on time and within budget. The advantage of this approach is that it means the project manager can concentrate on a relatively limited domain and can more readily deal with the trade-offs than if there are a large number of variables to follow. However, the issues with this approach may be that the project team does not directly seek to ensure that the business changes are being made that will maximise the benefits. Furthermore, changes may take place in the environment that mean that the IT product is no longer likely to deliver the anticipated benefits without modification.

CASE STUDY QUESTIONS

Review the case study on Foods. First you should gain an overview of the case (if not already done) and then focus in particular on the benefits stage. Where did the business benefits primarily come from? How was the focus maintained on the business benefits? What were the other goals of the programme and to what extent were they achieved?

SUMMARY

The chapter has covered the fifth and final stage of the IT-enabled business change life cycle. This stage of benefits delivery is ultimately the measure of success for the programme. Benefits should not be considered just at the start and the end of the programme. A continued focus is more likely to achieve the target and if necessary to move it (up or down) as the programme evolves. We have broadly covered the following topics.

TOPICS: BENEFITS MANAGEMENT

One of the most essential parts of any IT-enabled business change programme is to ensure that the benefits are identified and managed so that they are effectively delivered. This chapter studies the process of identifying, measuring and realising benefits. It covers:

- The types of benefits and relationship to basic accounting terms.
- The key financial benefits that are present in an investment appraisal.
- The types of non-financial benefits.
- Benefits measurement:
  - ✦ approaches to measuring benefits;
  - ✦ the concept of a balanced scorecard and its role in the measurement of benefits;
  - ✦ the definition of critical success factors and key performance indicators.
- Benefits realisation:
  - ✦ the definition of benefits realisation;
  - ✦ the objectives of a post-implementation review of benefits;
  - ✦ the need for actions to realise business benefits.

SAMPLE QUESTIONS

Question 36

What is always a characteristic of a KPI?

    (a) It is calculated using a computer system.

    (b) It is capable of being quantified.

    (c) It is applicable to all business functions.

    (d) It measures the performance of a manager.

Discussion

KPIs do not have to be calculated by a system nor do they have to be applicable across the whole of a business or measure management performance. While KPIs may do all of these things the one characteristic they must have is to be quantifiable.

Question 37

What do the initials CSF stand for?

    (a) Change solution factor.

    (b) Change success factor.

    (c) Critical success factor.

    (d) Critical solution factor.

Discussion

This is a straightforward question if you are familiar with the abbreviation CSF. The correct answer is (c) as the aim is to identify those factors which are most critical for success.

Question 38

Which of the following is **not** a type of tangible benefit?

    (a) Higher customer satisfaction.

    (b) Increased revenue.

    (c) Reduced working capital.

    (d) Lower fixed asset investment.

Discussion

A tangible benefit can be expressed directly in financial terms. All of the above except customer satisfaction fall into this category. It is possible for an executive such as the sales director to estimate a growth in revenue as a result of higher customer satisfaction; however, this is not a direct relationship that has been expressed here.

Question 39

Which of the following is an example of a tangible benefit?

    (a) Higher customer service level.

    (b) Headcount reduction.

    (c) Environmental improvement.

    (d) Greater employee satisfaction.

Discussion

This is a similar argument to the previous question. All of the above can be measured in some way but only the headcount reduction directly translates into a tangible benefit.

Question 40

What is the main purpose of tracking benefits?

    (a) Identify emerging opportunities to increase benefits.

    (b) Justify incentives to business sponsors.

    (c) Monitor benefits against expectations and targets.

    (d) Ensuring an accepted business case.

Discussion

Once a business case has been approved it is important to track the business benefits. While in some organisations certain stakeholders may be incentivised on benefits, the main reason is to compare benefits against the original targets and the revised expectations.

8 Skills and Techniques

Leadership and business change skills are at least as important as IT professional skills in delivering IT-enabled business change.

Jean Irvine, OBE, Change Leadership Network

GOALS

In this final chapter of the book there are some outstanding goals.

The first is to summarise the techniques for IT-enabled change that have been described in this book. Each of the techniques has been covered in the relevant chapter, hence this summary is primarily for the purpose of a review.

The techniques are categorised as change management and business modelling approaches. They are a valuable part of the toolbox for an IT-enabled business change professional. A related part of the armoury is to understand and gain the skills required to deliver successful IT-enabled business change.

Following the summary of techniques there is a section on skills which consolidates many of the identified business change and IT skills in relation to the SFIA. This is an opportunity to compare these skills with those present in your own organisation. The inclusion of these skills in version 3 of the SFIA model is a credit to the evolving discipline of IT-enabled business change.

There is a strong relationship between the jobs, roles and skills in an organisation. A job holder such as a business solutions manager may have different roles, for example business consultancy and account management. These roles will require different skills such as business analysis, consultancy and stakeholder management, which are described in the following section based on the SFIA definitions.

At several points in this book there have been references to a case study, which is based on a real-life situation. It is not often that an IT-enabled business change and alignment programme largely goes according to plan. That is not to say that there were not many challenges on the way. The description here is designed to pick out some salient learning points. For those of you that have not yet referred to this case study you can do so by reviewing the next chapter. The case is intended to illustrate many of the key points that have been explored in this book. It is based on real-life experiences but some elements such as the location and sector have been modified.

The *Glossary*, which can be found at the front of the book, contains a set of definitions associated with IT-enabled change. Understanding these definitions should be viewed as an important pre-requisite for gaining the qualification in IT-enabled business change. This glossary was created by the working party on IT-enabled business change and details of the contributors are shown in the *Acknowledgements.*

There is also a *Notes* section, which provides additional reference information as indicated with superscript numbers throughout the book. With the increasing amount of knowledge located on the web there are many other sources of information on IT-enabled business change.

SUMMARY OF TECHNIQUES

This book has covered a range of techniques. Below is a summary of these techniques grouped under the categories of change management and business modelling. Change management techniques are those that primarily support the transition of organisation and people into the new environment. Business modelling techniques are those that are designed to capture the current and target views of how the organisation delivers value.

In considering where to position the techniques this is to some extent a matter of judgement. Some have a good fit to one stage in the IT-enabled business change life cycle, others can be applied at multiple stages. The aim has been to find the 'centre-of-gravity', which is where the technique is most often applied.

Change management

Stakeholder relationship management was introduced early in this book in the chapter on business IT alignment. This was done because it is a technique that can, and should be, used at multiple points in the IT-enabled business change life cycle, not just at the implementation stage. Organisational and international culture was also introduced at this stage. The cultural aspects should certainly be covered in both the alignment and the implementation stages. Consultancy skills are required in multiple stages; however, there is a key focus in the business improvement stage where a high degree of expert advice and facilitation is needed. The degree of business change model was introduced to indicate the level of change assessed in the gap analysis part of the *Business Improvement* chapter, as were the techniques to elicit requirements.

The other change management techniques were described in the chapter on business change implementation, covering:

- force field analysis;
- unfreeze–transition–freeze;
- communication plans.

Business modelling

Business modelling has been used as an umbrella term to cover a range of techniques. Strategic analysis techniques are those that support the development of strategic alignment. These were covered in the *Business and IT Alignment* chapter and include:

- PESTLE;
- Value chain analysis;
- MOST;
- SWOT analysis.

In this book the elements of IT-enabled business change covered: organisation, people, process, information and technology. Enterprise architecture provides a big picture organisation view and was therefore covered in the *Business and IT Alignment* chapter.

There are techniques associated with each of the other areas. Much of the modelling supports business change design – in particular the people, process, information and technology dimensions of the business. The focus is on understanding both the current (as is) and future target (to be) views. In reviewing the people side, as well as the 'soft' elements of change management there is the modelling part of job design linked to work practice and task modelling. Business process and business information models were also covered in the design chapter, as was the IT requirements analysis.

TOPICS: TECHNIQUES

Business change techniques

The objective of this chapter is to provide the reader with an understanding of the best-practice techniques that are available to support IT-enabled business change. It examines the key techniques and how they can be applied to a business change programme. It includes:

- The principles of change management techniques:
    - force field analysis;
    - unfreeze–transition–freeze;
    - communications plans;
    - stakeholder relationship management;
    - consultancy skills and techniques;
    - business requirements elicitation and analysis.
- The identification, evaluation and selection of business change opportunities.
- The analysis of the impacts of proposed business changes.

- IT-enabled business change transformation.
- Analysis of organisational culture.
- Analysis of international cultures.

Business change in this context is used to mean dealing with the people aspects of change.

Business modelling and other techniques

There are modelling techniques for all the major elements of an IT-enabled business change programme and this part provides an overview of the key techniques. It covers:

- Business modelling techniques.
- Strategic analysis techniques.
- Organisational analysis and modelling.
- The dimensions/views of a business that may be modelled.
- Business process modelling and redesign.
- Task modelling.
- Information analysis and modelling.
- The key features of a business information model.
- IT requirements analysis and modelling.

ROLES AND SKILLS FRAMEWORK

A significant number of roles have been identified in this book which required a wide range of skills needed to operate across the IT-enabled business change life cycle. This section describes these skills using a widely accepted skills framework.

SFIA is the Skills Framework for the Information Age. In this third version, there is a much greater focus on business change skills. Table 8.1 maps selected skills onto the different stages of the IT-enabled change life cycle. It is the author's assessment of this mapping and readers may wish to review the whole SFIA framework to decide what is relevant for their organisations.

The first column (0) is a generic skill across the life cycle. Other skills may also be used across the life cycle but have been positioned here in a stage of the life cycle that is considered appropriate. This should be regarded as a guide. The stages are:

(1) alignment;
(2) improvement;
(3) design;
(4) implementation;
(5) benefits.

TABLE 8.1   *SFIA skills mapped to IT-enabled business change lifecycle*

	Stage					
Skill	**0**	**1**	**2**	**3**	**4**	**5**
Stakeholder relationship management	X					
Programme management	X					
Strategic planning		X				
Innovation		X				
Business analysis			X			
Systems architecture			X			
Organisation design and implementation				X		
Business process improvement				X		
Information management				X		
Systems development management				X		
Project management				X		
Business process testing					X	
Systems testing					X	
Change implementation planning and management					X	
Change management					X	
Benefits management						X
Service-level management						X

The details for each of these skills are shown on the SFIA website. At this site access is available to the description of each level of skill. This demonstrates how staff can professionally progress in the area of business change. It will be seen that all the skills have been selected from the business change category and some have been selected from the large number of IT skills.

Below, the headline definitions are given, with kind permission from the SFIA Foundation.

Stakeholder management

The co-ordination of relationships with and between key stakeholders, during the design, management and implementation of business change.

Programme management

The identification, planning and co-ordination of a set of related projects within a programme of business change, to manage their interdependencies in support of specific business strategies. Maintains a strategic view over the set of projects, providing the framework for implementing business initiatives, or large-scale change, by achieving a vision of the outcome of the programme. The vision, and the means of achieving it, may change as the programme progresses.

Strategic planning

The development or review of an information systems strategy to support an organisation's business goals and the development of plans to drive forward and manage that strategy. Working with others to embed the strategic management of information systems as part of the management of the organisation.

Innovation

The capability to recognise and exploit business opportunities provided by IT (for example, the internet), to ensure more efficient and effective performance of organisations, to explore possibilities for new ways of conducting business and organisational processes and to establish new businesses.

Business analysis

The methodical investigation, analysis, review and documentation of all or part of a business in terms of business functions and processes, the information used and the data on which the information is based. The definition of requirements for improving any aspect of the processes and systems and quantification of potential business benefits. The creation of viable specifications and acceptance criteria in preparation for the construction of information and communication systems.

Systems architecture

The specification of systems architectures, identifying the components needed to meet the present and future requirements, both functional and non-functional (such as security), of the business as a whole, and the interrelationships between these components. The provision of direction and guidance on all technical aspects of the development of, and modifications to, information systems to ensure that they take account of relevant architectures, strategies, policies, standards and practices and that existing and planned systems and IT infrastructure remain compatible.

(Note: this description could be expanded to include other enterprise architecture responsibilities such as information architecture.)

Business process improvement

The identification of new and alternative approaches to performing business activities. The analysis of business processes, including recognition of the potential for automation of the processes, assessment of the costs and potential benefits of the new approaches considered and, where appropriate, management of change and assistance with implementation.

Information management

The overall management of information, as a fundamental business resource, to ensure that the information needs of the business are met. Encompasses development and promotion of the strategy and policies covering the design of information structures and taxonomies, the setting of policies for the sourcing and maintenance of the data content, the management and storage of electronic content and the analysis of information structure (including logical analysis of data and metadata). Includes overall responsibility for compliance with regulations, standards and codes of good practice relating to information and documentation records management, information assurance and data protection.

Organisation design

The design of organisation structure, role profiles, culture, performance measurement, competencies and skills, to support strategies for change and for training to enable the change. Identification of key attributes of the culture and key principles and factors for addressing location strategy.

Systems development management

The management of resources in order to plan, estimate and carry out programmes of systems development work to time, budget and quality targets and in accordance with appropriate standards.

Project management

The management of projects, typically (but not exclusively) involving the development and implementation of business processes to meet identified business needs, acquiring and utilising the necessary resources and skills, within agreed parameters of cost, timescales and quality.

Change implementation planning and management

Defining and managing the process of deploying and integrating IT capabilities into the business in a way that is sensitive to, and fully compatible with, business operations.

Change management

The management of all changes to the components of a live infrastructure, from requests for change (RFC) through to implementation and review, to support the continued availability, effectiveness and safety of the infrastructure.

Business process testing

The planning, design, management, execution and reporting of business process tests and usability evaluations. The application of evaluation skills to the assessment of the ergonomics, usability and fitness for purpose of defined processes. This includes the synthesis of test tasks to be performed (from statement of user needs and user interface specification), the design of an evaluation programme, the selection of user samples, the analysis of performance and inputting results to the development team.

Systems testing

The planning, design, management, execution and reporting of tests, using appropriate testing tools and techniques and conforming to agreed standards, to ensure that new and amended systems, together with any interfaces, perform as specified.

Benefits management

Monitoring for the emergence of anticipated policy benefits (typically specified as part of the business case for a change programme or project). Action (typically by the programme management team) to optimise the business impact of individual and combined benefits.

Service-level management

The planning, implementation and control of service provision. This includes negotiation, implementation and monitoring of service-level agreements, and the ongoing management of operational facilities to provide the agreed levels of service, seeking continuously and proactively to improve service delivery.

CIO ROLE AND SKILLS

The enhanced focus of SFIA version 3 on business change skills emphasises the need for IT managers to broaden their own skills and those of their direct reports. Research by the author has demonstrated that this requirement is being recognised by the top IS managers in organisations. The following is a modified extract from a report on this research.

From IT manager to CIO – a research input

What is the primary role of an IT manager? Is it to manage the technology and operational services or is it to drive IT-enabled business change? The term 'CIO' is more likely to be used for someone who does the latter, although if the former is not being managed, it is difficult if not impossible to establish credibility in a change role. What transforms a technology manager into a real CIO who is regarded as an effective influencer of strategy – someone who makes the organisation significantly more effective in reaching its objectives?

This does not require greater technical knowledge or even project management skills. What it needs is a shift in focus, both organisationally and personally, from technology management to technology exploitation. A typical technology manager works on the sourcing, installation, deployment and management of IT systems, both hardware and software. This is vital. The introduction of technology presents many traps and good IT managers avoid those traps to deliver efficiency and responsiveness. However, technology does not by itself drive agility or a customer focus, or progress to any other business goal.

By contrast CIOs are expected to be forward-looking managers, focused on IT exploitation, who work in the overlap between strategy, technology and organisation. They find creative ways in which their organisations can improve, and occasionally transform, business processes and information exchange. They view technology as just one of the enablers.

Progressing from a production to a customer focus means a different relationship with the rest of the business. The IT culture has to switch from a tell to a sell approach. Those who make a successful transition earn the credibility to move into a partnership mode.

Henley Management College and the BCS conducted a survey of over 50 senior IT figures to determine which skills they viewed as important and which they perceived to be lacking in their industry. Half of the respondents were responsible for budgets of more than £5 million.

The survey categorised five different types of skills in the IT arena: technical, professional, management, business and personal. Responses confirmed the distinctive nature of the five skills. A key research output is that the skills required to support the change in focus and exploit IT – those skills most needed to transfer from being an IT Manager to a CIO – are both scarce and prized by IT directors.

Technical skills are not the problem. Just 2% of respondents said that their organisation lacked IT managers with the right technical skills (for example, developing Oracle databases and supporting Microsoft operating systems). Developing professional skills in areas such as service and project management is considered more important than maintaining technical skills. Yet responses show that these are not the major barrier to an IT manager's progress to senior management.

One might expect that the organisations interviewed – many of them large businesses – would be able to recruit and develop the skills needed to manage the implementation of technology. Yet there was a surprising and substantial gap in management skills, highlighted by 41% of respondents. Senior IT directors said that the big challenge is to find the people who combine technical and managerial skills with the human skills needed to get the best out of people.

Supporting this finding, the most critical of the five skill needs was personal skills that enable IT managers to gain the respect of non-IT executives and to build effective partnerships. Fifty-three per cent of IT heads indicated that there was a shortage of people with a high level of personal skills, such as communication and leadership.

One respondent said that he wanted managers who had 'Personality – and the ability to interrelate with colleagues within IT and elsewhere in the business.' Another commented that 'Communications skills at all levels are utterly essential – particularly listening skills.'

A similar number, 51%, said they were lacking in knowledge of business, both in general and in their industry, and the ability to apply this knowledge to real situations. For instance, one IT director wanted 'someone who always thinks about alignment with business goals and objectives.' Another emphasised 'hybrid skills – being able to connect IT and business.'

In summary, it is clear that IT managers cannot ignore technical, professional and managerial skills in building IT capability. However, without strong personal and business skills they and their direct reports have little hope of operating in the strategic space of exploiting IT capability that leads to the CIO role in an organisation.

A version of this research summary was reported in *Computer Weekly* **in an article by Sharm Manwani and David Flint on 2 November 2004.**

CIO AND ORGANISATIONAL CAPABILITY ROLES

The CIO may or may not have a role in IT-enabled business change that relates directly to a given programme. What is vital, however, is that the CIO has a focus on raising the organisation's capability to implement change programmes over a period of time.

A CIO may be part of the sponsoring group for a large programme that impacts upon the success of the organisation. Additionally, a role of the CIO is to create an effective environment for business change and to ensure that the major change programmes are aligned to the strategic goals. A forward-thinking CIO who has credibility with the top team will be actively engaged in making this happen, particularly for, but not necessarily exclusively for, IT-enabled change programmes. A CIO who has been able to demonstrate the ability to deliver business IT projects on time and within budget may be asked to take on a broader role. One way for the CIO to encourage this to happen is to carry out an audit of the organisation's capability to manage change.

Organisational capability maturity

In addition to the skills required by an individual project manager there is the question of the overall organisation capability. Organisations have differing degrees of capability in managing projects, programmes and the overall portfolio.

The OGC has created a maturity model to assess this capability. This has five levels, which is the same as many other capability maturity models and the following questions support the evaluation.

Level 1 – initial process

Does the organisation recognise projects and run them differently from its ongoing business? (Projects may be run informally with no standard process or tracking system.)

Level 2 – repeatable process

Does the organisation ensure that each project is run with its own processes and procedures to a minimum specified standard? (There may be limited consistency or co-ordination between projects.)

Level 3 – defined process

Does the organisation have its own centrally controlled project processes, and can individual projects flex within these processes to suit the particular project?

Level 4 – managed process

Does the organisation obtain and retain specific measurements on its project management performance and run a quality management organisation to better predict future performance?

Level 5 – optimised process

POINT TO PONDER

What level of organisational capability in project management does your organisation, or one that you know well, possess? Is there a plan in place to enhance this capability?

Does the organisation run continuous process improvement with proactive problem and technology management for projects in order to improve its ability to depict performance over time and optimise processes?

CONCLUSIONS

I trust that the readers of this book recognise that there are no simple answers to the question of how to make large IT-enabled business change programmes successful. If there were it would be unusual to see programmes where large amounts of money have been spent without a return on investment. On the other hand, analyses of both successes and failures have concluded that following good practice is more likely to lead to success and that the inverse is also true.

Whatever your role or reason for learning about IT-enabled business change, I hope that you have taken away some insights from this journey. Equally, I hope that the messages in this book stimulate you to think about what successful IT-enabled business change means in your organisations and how you can help achieve it.

Case Study

An illustrative case study drawn from the author's real-life experiences.

IT-ENABLED CHANGE CASE STUDY

The following case illustrates the breadth and complexity of an IT-enabled change programme with a sequence that follows the five stages of the IT-enabled change model. It demonstrates how business processes were redesigned and an ERP package was selected and implemented in a major subsidiary of a multinational company.

The case identifies:

- the strategic context;
- the alignment process and the drivers for change;
- the business improvement initiatives;
- designing the change;
- implementing the design;
- benefits of the programme;
- case lessons.

Strategic context

At the start of the case Foods was one of the largest independent manufacturing and distribution drinks companies in Spain, employing more than 1000 people. It was acquired by the Group, who integrated Foods into the multinational organisation using their standard business model. As a consequence Foods was restructured to distribute both its existing products and also the Group brands in Spain while manufacturing and marketing its products to the international market. This multidivision structure resulted in increased size and complexity.

The company had been formed by the owner and his family, who had run Foods with a centralised top-down (power) culture. With the acquisition by the Group the family left the organisation and new executives with Spanish and international experience were recruited to support and direct the existing management team in implementing this change.

What were the business and IT drivers for change in the alignment process?

The restructuring of Foods in effect created a new business model with a national (Spanish) sales company, an international brand company and a production company for both domestic and export markets. During the early stages of the acquisition of Foods the Group IT director initiated an audit of the IT systems. This exposed a lack of information flows between people, processes and systems resulting from the previous power culture of the organisation in which all major decisions were made by the owner.

In this new Group-controlled environment, procedures, controls and reporting became more important. This required a different type of culture combined with new business and systems capabilities. However, with a new team and given the history of individual as opposed to team decisions the way forward was not clear. It was agreed that there was an urgent need to identify which business process changes would provide the tangible benefits desired by the Group as part of its financial acquisition goals.

The audit had highlighted that the existing systems comprised a mixture of bespoke developments and application packages running on a mid-range computer which had significant performance problems. There was poor integration between systems resulting in additional data entry and potential errors from the unnecessary human interface. Statutory accounting for Spain was supported but not the range of management reports needed in a multinational company. Sales and marketing systems were limited to diverse PC spreadsheets. Physical stock did not automatically match stock accounting. There was no facility to measure customer service levels. Sales forecasting was a problem both in terms of accuracy and in the absence of a consistent volume, production and financial forecast.

Although these information problems were considered serious by the Group, the management team in Spain did not see the full impact of these issues. One reason for this was that the previous owner had run the company on hierarchical lines with managers rewarded primarily for their functional skills and their loyalty.

It was important to identify a senior-level sponsor who understood that there were issues and opportunities that needed to be addressed in the Spanish organisation. In this case it was the newly appointed finance director (FD) who had been sent to the subsidiary by Head Office in order to enhance the financial results of the acquired company. One advantage was that this target provided a direct reason for him to support the necessary business changes. Furthermore he worked closely with the Spanish managing director (MD), who had wide international experience and had been recruited especially for this role.

The FD and MD agreed with the Group IT director to run an alignment workshop with the company management to evaluate what the opportunities might be from changing the business processes and supporting these where needed with new systems. At this point there were no preconceptions of the outcomes from this process.

Scoping the business improvement initiatives

Following the above decision a two-day Executive Information Planning (EIP) session was initiated by the Group IT director in order to clarify and respond to the business and systems change drivers. This off-site retreat was viewed and planned as a means to brainstorm improvements in business processes and new uses of information systems. An independent consultant was hired to facilitate the event using a proven methodology. Before the workshop the list of high-level business processes was agreed with the FD.

The session reviewed each of the business processes and observed a strict methodology, setting specific tasks for each process. These were:

- define the problems;
- quantify the benefits from resolving the problems;
- identify the requirements to solve the problems;
- assess what part of the requirement depended on improved systems.

The managers were asked to highlight the problems in the company and to assess the impact both on themselves and on other managers involved in the same business process. For example, an inaccurate and constantly changing sales forecast reduced manufacturing efficiency and had a negative impact on responding to customer demands as well as making it difficult to accurately predict the company revenues.

As a result of the workshop, many initiatives were identified with large potential benefits, half of which depended on new information systems. The potential savings were more than £8 million from improving business processes such as increasing logistics responsiveness to market changes and avoidance of duplicate work due to unconnected systems. A set of initiatives was agreed at the workshop. Managers were given responsibility for analysing each process initiative under the guidance of a steering committee.

It was evident from an initial analysis that the consolidated set of requirements to support the new cross-functional processes could not be met by modifying the existing systems. The alternative of redeveloping the systems would take far longer than purchasing an application package providing the fit to the requirements was high enough. Sufficient analysis was done to verify that there was at least one ERP which would meet the criteria. Using some broad assumptions high-level costs were estimated.

The benefits were clearly shown to outweigh the business costs and this formed the basis of the business case that was approved by local management and which then needed to go to the Group Executive Board. Approval was not a quick process since the Group had doubts about the ability of the local organisation to deliver such a radical change. In the meantime work commenced on designing the business change, which had the dual advantage of continuing the project and providing further support for the business case. The Group did give the go-ahead for the programme while specifying that there should be approval gates to release the funds based on delivery.

Designing the business change

Each team analysed the outputs of the EIP, expanding the requirements and confirming the benefits. The sales forecasting process exemplifies the business improvements through sharing of structured information between different parts of the value chain. Originally sales, production and finance all had separate volume forecasts. Sales management set ambitious targets internally for its sales force to encourage greater effort and performance. They gave a smaller but still high figure to production relative to real expectation in order to reduce the risk that they would be short of stock. At the same time they provided a lower figure than expected to finance for the budget forecast so that their financial goals would not be so tough. Production and finance did not believe the sales figure and therefore set their own numbers. Changes in the forecasts were not communicated between departments. This led to increased stock, lost sales and inaccurate financial predictions.

When this situation was recognised at the workshop, after a tough discussion the management team agreed that the process needed to be redesigned. The new process was designed to be built on the output of a cross-functional team forecast supported by an improved sales history and planning system. Information sharing and trust between the functions were the key success factors. This was not an easy change but top management had seen the effects of the old process and were determined to change the culture of separate working.

In summary, the design of the business change required an enhanced structure, people process, information and technology components to work in a harmonised manner. The programme design reflected this need. Each project in the programme was assigned an executive sponsor and business project manager with systems management support. The teams who had conducted the initial analysis were supplemented with business and IT staff who had detailed knowledge of the business processes and information systems.

Implementation of the design

The detailed requirements of the 'to be' processes then formed the basis of the next stage. The Group policy was to buy, not develop, systems where feasible. A product and supplier evaluation was therefore conducted for the new systems. Before this process a shortlist of suppliers was created based on key criteria selected by the programme team with the support of the Group IT director. Suppliers needed to have industry knowledge, international experience and to meet local statutory accounting regulations. There was a strong desire for a single supplier for all of the systems; however, it was recognised that it might not be possible to both meet this goal and also achieve a high fit of functionality to business requirements. In the end a compromise solution was chosen such that the sales and production business units had application packages from two international suppliers but using a single local Spanish partner to provide implementation support, including the required system interfaces.

A decision needed to be taken on whether to go for a 'big bang' or an incremental approach to introducing the new systems. The 'big bang' solution would save time and effort in writing interfaces from the new to the old systems, which were required in the phased approach. However, since every major system in the organisation needed to be changed, a 'big bang' solution was considered to be too risky by local and Group management.

The first set of functionality to be introduced was the financial accounting suite. This had the advantage that the users were relatively IT literate and there were fewer process changes than in other areas, although still significant changes in the management accounting that would bring substantial benefits. The financial systems were implemented on time and within budget. Benefits were confirmed by the post-implementation review, which provided the credibility for the further investment. Following this promising start, the sales and production processes and systems were implemented as planned with relatively minor revisions. Recognising that the changes were substantial, the local management informed all customers of the improvement plan and managed their expectations to protect and enhance the benefits.

Realising the benefits

The overall programme had three main goals:

- Achieve the quantified business benefits from addressing the process issues.
- Implement a new flexible systems infrastructure to support the process changes.
- Create a team-working culture that would facilitate the programme and also support the move to a multinational and multidivision philosophy.

The project identified, tracked and realised substantial business and IT benefits that were in line with the business case. In the words of the FD, 'Foods has up and running an integrated solution across all functions.' This programme had a committed management team that recognised the need for change and planned it in an organised manner. The integrated systems plan with quantified benefits maintained the momentum of the change programme and created a sustainable platform.

During the first part of the programme both the MD and the FD played an active role in driving through the process changes that were needed to deliver the benefits. After the first implementation, the MD was promoted to a Group role and the local marketing director was promoted to MD. Fortunately, he was equally supportive of the programme. The Group IT director played an active part throughout the change programme in advising local management and engaging with Group stakeholders to keep the focus on the Group goals.

Case lessons

The case study illustrates many of the advantages and potential pitfalls in implementing IT-enabled business change. A thorough analysis of process and data requirements avoided the assumption that a purchased systems package is an automatic fit. Areas that do not fit well need a change in process (potential resistance), an adaptation of software (giving high cost or risk) or integration with another package (causing time and data problems).

Senior management commitment was high at the start of the programme and was maintained all the way through. It was fortunate that both the MD and the FD were in place for the critical first implementation and that when the MD was succeeded by the marketing director continuity of support was maintained. This team plus the Group IT director ensured that all the stakeholders were engaged, including local staff, suppliers, customers and the Group.

The methodology used to deliver the programme was subsequently applied in other parts of the Group. However, this particular implementation in Spain remained the best example of a holistic approach to IT-enabled business change.

Notes

1. See the description of the Standish Report on IT projects at http://www.softwaremag.com/L.cfm?Doc=newsletter/2004-01-15/Standish

2. This research was conducted by Tim O'Leary and Sharm Manwani and supported by the Change Leadership Network and Serco.

3. See report from National Audit Office at http://www.nao.org.uk/publications/nao_reports/06-07/060733_SROdatatables.pdf

4. The Office of Government Commerce provides a range of advice and tools that is relevant to IT-enabled business change. See www.ogc.gov.uk

5. PRINCE2 is a process-based methodology for project management. See www.ogc.gov.uk/methods_prince_2.asp

6. The SFIA framework is accessible via www.sfia.org.uk

7. Michael Porter wrote ground-breaking books on strategic competitive advantage that introduce key frameworks such as generic strategies, five forces and value chain. See Porter (1980, 1985).

8. See IT Governance Institute at http://www.itgi.org/

9. For further information on TOGAF see the Open Group website at http://www.opengroup.org/architecture/togaf8-doc/arch/

10. There are many diagrammatic representations of the Zachman framework available on the internet, for example http://www.zachmaninternational.com/fwgraphic.html

11. Source: www.outsourcing.com – Outsourcing Essentials – vol. 3, no. 4, 2005.

12. Soft systems methodology is an approach to analysing business situations devised by Peter Checkland and his team at Lancaster University.

13. The ISEB Consultancy syllabus is at http://www.bcs.org/server.php?show=nav.7175

14. Six Sigma details can be found at http://www.isixsigma.com/sixsigma/six_sigma.asp

15. IMP is the Information Management Professionals group and it has promoted an integrated approach to information management.

16. An OGC review of development methods can be viewed at http://www.ogc.gov.uk/delivery_life cycle_application_development_modularity.asp

17. See the description of Lewin's model by Edgar Schein at http://www.solonline.org/res/wp/10006.html

References

Carnall, C. A. (1999) *Managing change in organizations.* Pearson Education Ltd, Harlow.

Deal, T. E. and Kennedy, A. A. (1982) *Corporate cultures: The rites and rituals of corporate life.* Penguin Books, Harmondsworth.

Hamel, G. and Prahalad, C.K. (1990) The core competence of the corporation. *Harv. Bus. Rev.*, 68(3), 79–91.

Handy, C. B. (1993) *Understanding organisations*, 4th edn. Penguin Books, Harmondsworth.

Hofstede, G. (2001) *Culture's consequences, comparing values, behaviors, institutions, and organizations across nations.* Sage Publications, Thousand Oaks, CA.

Kaplan, R. and Norton, D. (1996) *Translating strategy into action: The balanced scorecard.* Harvard Business School Press, Boston, MA.

Manwani, S. (2007) Keeping both sides happy. *Computing Business*, 15 February.

Paul, D. and Yeates, D. (eds) (2006) *Business analysis.* British Computer Society, Swindon.

Porter, M. (1980) *Competitive strategy.* Free Press, New York.

Porter, M. (1985) *Competitive advantage.* Free Press, New York.

Rockart, J. F. (1979) Chief executives define their own data needs. *Harv. Bus. Rev.*, March–April, 81–92.

Schein, E. H. (1965) *Organizational psychology* (2nd edn, 1970; 3rd edn, 1980). Prentice-Hall, Englewood Cliffs, NJ.

Venkatraman, N. (1994) IT-enabled business transformation: from automation to business scope redefinition. *Sloan Manag. Rev.*, Winter, 73–87.

Ward, J. and Peppard, J. (2002) *Strategic planning for information systems*, 3rd edn. Wiley, Chichester, UK.

Index